NOTES ON

COUNTY COURT

PRACTICE AND PROCEDURE

by HUGH C. COLLINS, LL.B.

Chief Clerk, Birmingham County Court
Editor of "Humphreys' Notes on District Registry
Practice and Procedure" and
"Humphreys' Notes on Matrimonial Causes
Proceeding in District Registries"

THIRD EDITION

LONDON
Oyez Publishing

©
OYEZ PUBLISHING LIMITED
OYEZ HOUSE, BREAMS BUILDINGS
FETTER LANE, LONDON, EC4P 4BU
1974

SBN 85120 130   X

First edition	. . . . .	*May,* 1967
Second edition	. . . .	*March,* 1972
Revised and reprinted	. . . .	*October,* 1972
Third Edition	. . . . .	*January,* 1974

MADE AND PRINTED IN GREAT BRITAIN BY
PAGE BROS (NORWICH) LTD.

PREFACE

The main object of this book is to help solicitors and their staffs and plaintiffs in person to determine a point of county court procedure quickly. Also, it appears that the book is used for training purposes, by Citizens' Advice Bureaux and court staffs. One hopes that all these needs are met as far as possible within the compass of the new edition.

It has been found in practice that it is useful to include notes on the commencement of proceedings authorised by various statutes, such as matters within the Companies Act, 1948, outside winding-up jurisdiction, and matters under the statutes affecting landlord and tenant, without too much detail which would lengthen the book. The information is such as to help when proceedings have to be taken urgently and there is little time for research. The requirements on issue are so often the only key that is needed.

The Act referred to in this book is the County Courts Act, **1959, the Orders and Rules** referred to are the County Court Rules, 1936, as amended, unless otherwise stated, and **the Forms** are those in Appendix A to these Rules, unless otherwise stated. The number after the fees is that of the fee in the County Court Fees Order, 1971. Companion books deal with divorce proceedings and bankruptcy proceedings.

The word *"præcipe"* has been used in several places instead of the new term "request" to make the meaning clear in as few words as possible and to avoid ambiguity. Where the word *"præcipe"* is used, there is no doubt that it refers to the prescribed form required to be completed and filed in court in order to commence proceedings.

The widened procedure of arbitration for "consumer" claims is described.

H.C.C.

CONTENTS

NOTES ON COUNTY COURT PRACTICE AND PROCEDURE

GENERAL

THE present county courts were first set up under the County Courts Act, 1846. They replaced the old county courts and local courts. County court districts originally were planned on a county basis, but the 1846 Act allowed the districts to be varied without requiring their boundaries to coincide with the county. The epithet, county, is a misnomer.

The basic enactment regulating county courts is the County Courts Act, 1959, and the rules thereunder are the County Court Rules, 1936 (S.R. & O., 1936, No. 626), as amended. There are other Acts and rules regulating business in county courts.

Some county courts have jurisdiction under the Matrimonial Causes Act, 1967, for the issue of proceedings in divorce and annulment of marriages. These are dealt with in a companion volume to this book.

A list of county courts, with the relevant Admiralty and bankruptcy courts, and their telephone numbers appears at the end of the *County Court Practice*.

The places in the respective county court districts are listed in two books published by H.M. Stationery Office, "Index to the Parishes, etc., in Districts of County Courts" and "London County Court Directory".

County courts are civil courts, which, except in minor instances, are staffed by civil servants of the Lord Chancellor's Department. The judicial officers are judges and registrars. Circuit judges are assigned to sit in county courts (Courts Act, 1971, s. 20). No person is qualified to be registrar or assistant registrar unless he is a solicitor of at least seven years standing (s. 21 (1) of the Act). Registrars are comparable to masters in the High Court.

The chief clerk is responsible for the administration of a county court (*Ord*. 48, *r*. 26).

JURISDICTION

County Courts Act, 1959

County courts may hear and determine:—

(1) Actions founded on *contract and tort* where amount claimed is not more than £750, but excluding libel and slander (s. 39). See also jurisdiction under the Hire-Purchase Act, 1965, *infra*.

(2) Actions to recover *penalty*, expenses, contribution or other like demand under any enactment, if it is not recoverable only in some other court, and if the amount claimed does not exceed £750, but not a fine on indictment or summary conviction (s. 40).

(3) Actions for the *recovery of land* where the net annual value for rating does not exceed £1,000 (s. 48). The limit of jurisdiction is the same for forfeiture of a lease under the Law of Property Act, 1925, s. 146 (s. 52 and Sched. I to the Act). Where the land does not consist of hereditaments having a separate net annual value for rating, the land is taken to have a net annual value for rating equal to its value by the year, but shall not be taken to have a net annual value for rating exceeding that of any hereditament of which it forms part (s. 200 (2)).

The Rent Act, 1968, s. 105, gives jurisdiction to county courts where this Act applies, and, in certain cases, notwithstanding that any amount claimed would not otherwise be within the jurisdiction of a county court. Since the 1st April 1973, the limits of Rent Act jurisdiction is £1,500 in Greater London and £750 elsewhere.

Where a mortgage includes a dwelling-house and no part of the land is situated in Greater London, if a county court has jurisdiction to determine an action for possession of the mortgaged property under the County Courts Act, 1959, s. 48, the county court has exclusive jurisdiction unless the action is for foreclosure or sale in which a claim for possession is also made (Administration of Justice Act, 1970, s. 37). This section applies even if a claim is also made for payment of an amount due under the mortgage exceeding the county court's jurisdiction (*ibid.* s. 38).

(4) Actions in which the *title to any hereditament* comes into question, and which would otherwise be within the jurisdiction (*a*) in the case of an easement or licence, if the net annual value for rating of the hereditament in respect of which, or on, through, over or under which the easement or license is claimed does not exceed £1000, or (*b*) in any other case, if the net annual value for rating of the hereditament does not exceed £1000 (s. 51).

Except by consent of the parties, the county court does not have jurisdiction in an action in which the title to any toll, fair, market or franchise is in question (s. 39 (1)).

(5) *Equity proceedings* (s. 52)—all the jurisdiction of the High Court in the following proceedings:—

(*a*) for the *administration of the estate of a deceased person*, where the estate does not exceed in amount or value £5,000; the limit would appear to be the value of the deceased's *net* estate, *cf.* Family Provision Act, 1966, s. 7 (1).

(*b*) for the execution of any *trust* or for a declaration that a trust subsists or proceedings under the Variation of Trusts Act, 1958, s. 1, where the estate or fund subject, or alleged to be subject, to the trust does not exceed in amount or value £5,000;

(*c*) for foreclosure or redemption of any *mortgage* or for enforcing any charge or lien, where the amount owing in respect of the mortgage, charge or lien does not exceed £5,000;

(*d*) for the *specific performance*, or for the *rectification*, delivery up or cancellation, of any agreement for the sale, purchase or lease of any property, where, in the case of a sale or purchase, the purchase money, or in the case of a lease, the value of the property, does not exceed £5,000;

(*e*) relating to the *maintenance or advancement of an infant*, where the property of the infant does not exceed £5,000;

(*f*) for the dissolution or winding up of any *partnership* (whether or not the existence of the partnership is in dispute), where the whole assets of the partnership do not exceed in amount or value £5,000;

(*g*) for *relief against fraud or mistake* where the damage sustained or the estate or fund in respect of which relief is sought does not exceed £5,000.

Under s. 52 (3) of the Act, equity jurisdiction is given under certain sections of a number of enactments set out in Sched. I to the Act, limited to the amounts therein stated, usually £5,000, or net annual value for rating of £300 or £1,000 depending upon the enactment.

The enactments, without stating the relevant sections, are as follows:—

Trustee Act, 1925;
Law of Property Act, 1925;
Land Charges Act, 1925;
Administration of Estates Act, 1925;
Leasehold Property (Repairs) Act, 1938.

Under the Trustee Act, 1925, s. 63, for instance, money may be paid into court, or securities, or debt or thing in action, as the case may be, where the amount or value does not exceed £5,000. Under the Law of Property Act, 1925, s. 146, which relates to restrictions on and relief against forfeiture of leases for breach of a covenant or condition, the county court has jurisdiction where the net annual value for rating of the property comprised in the lease does not exceed £1,000.

(6) *Admiralty.*—Certain county courts have jurisdiction in Admiralty under s. 55 of the Act. These courts are listed at the end of the *County Court Practice*. Where a court has such jurisdiction, the parts of the sea, if any, adjacent to the district assigned to it to a distance of three miles from the shore are deemed to be included in its district (s. 55 (2)).

These courts have jurisdiction to hear and determine any of the following claims, if the claim does not exceed £1,000 (except in the case of *salvage*, in which case the courts have jurisdiction where the value of the property saved does not exceed £3,500). The claims are (s. 56 (1))—

(*a*) for *damage done* by a ship;

(*b*) for *damage received* by a ship;

(*c*) for *loss of life or personal injury* sustained in consequence of any defect in a ship or in her apparel or equipment, or of the wrongful act, neglect or default of the owners, charterers or persons in possession or control of a ship or of a master or crew thereof or of any other person for whose wrongful acts, neglects or defaults the owners, charterers or persons in possession or control of a ship are responsible, being an act, neglect or default in the navigation or management of the ship, in the loading, carriage or discharge of goods on, in or from the ship or in the embarkation, carriage or disembarkation of persons on, in or from the ship;

(*d*) for *loss of or damage to goods carried in a ship*;

(*e*) arising out of any agreement relating to the *carriage of goods* in a ship or to the *use or hire* of a ship;

(*f*) in the nature of *salvage* (including any claim under the Civil Aviation Act, 1949, relating to salvage to aircraft, their apparel and cargo) (in this case the limit of jurisdiction is £3,500);

(*g*) in the nature of *towage* in respect of a ship or aircraft;

(*h*) in the nature of *pilotage* in respect of ship or aircraft;

(*j*) in respect of *goods or materials supplied* to a ship for her operation or maintenance;

(*k*) in respect of the *construction, repairs, or equipment* of a ship or *dock charges* or dues;

(*l*) by a master or member of the crew for *wages*;

(*m*) by a master, shipper, charterer or agent in respect of *disbursements* made on account of a ship.

As to hovercraft, see the Hovercraft Act, 1968, s. 2.

(7) *Probate.*—A county court has jurisdiction in a contentious matter where the value of the estate is less than £1,000 exclusive of what the deceased was possessed of or entitled to as a trustee and not beneficially, but after making allowance for funeral expenses and for debts and incumbrances; ss. 62 to 64 of the Act apply.

(8) *Counterclaims.*—Where any counterclaim, or set-off and counterclaim, involves matter beyond the jurisdiction of a county court, any party may apply to the High Court for an order that the whole proceedings or the proceedings on the counterclaim or set-off be transferred to the High Court (s. 65 (1)). The application must be made, by the plaintiff within eight days of the receipt of counterclaim, and by the party counterclaiming within eight days of filing the counterclaim (R.S.C., *Ord.* 107, *r.* 2).

The High Court may order either—

(a) that the whole proceedings be transferred to the High Court; or

(b) that the whole proceedings be heard and determined in the county court; or

(c) that the counterclaim or set-off and counterclaim be transferred to the High Court and that the proceedings on the plaintiff's claim and defence thereto other than the set-off (if any) be heard and determined in the county court (s. 65 (2)).

If no application is made within the prescribed time, or if it is ordered that the whole proceedings be heard and determined in the county court, the county court will have jurisdiction (s. 65 (3)).

(9) *Ancillary jurisdiction.*—A county court may, in the proceedings before it—

(a) grant such relief, redress or remedy or combination of remedies, either absolute or conditional; and

(b) give such and the like effect to every ground of defence or counterclaim equitable or legal,

as ought to be granted or given by the High Court and in as full and ample a manner (s. 74).

A *declaration or injunction* may not be granted unless it is claimed or applied for as ancillary to a claim otherwise within the jurisdiction, or, in a few instances, some enactment gives the necessary power. A county court has power to make a declaration under s. 43A of the Landlord and Tenant Act, 1954, for instance. For the extent of this jurisdiction the reported cases are referred to in notes after s. 74 of the County

Courts Act, 1959, in the *County Court Practice* 1973, at p. 76 and also at p. 35.

An order for *specific delivery of goods* may be made, for the county court has jurisdiction in detinue (which is a tort) within the limits of its jurisdiction.

(10) *Replevin.*—Actions of replevin are rare; ss. 104 to 106 of the Act apply.

(11) *Jurisdiction by consent or agreement.*—Jurisdiction under the County Courts Act, 1959, is extended in certain cases by agreement.

In an action which could have been assigned to the *Queen's Bench*, if the parties agree by a memorandum signed by them or their solicitors that a county court specified in the memorandum shall have jurisdiction, that court will have power to hear and determine it (s. 42).

In *Equity* proceedings (that is, those proceedings in which a county court would have jurisdiction, but for the limitation of amount, under the County Courts Act, 1959, s. 52, or under the Settled Land Act, 1925, s. 113 (3), but not under the Variation of Trusts Act, 1958, s. 1), if the parties agree by a memorandum signed by them or their solicitors or agents that a county court specified in the memorandum shall have jurisdiction, that court will have power to hear and determine it (s. 53).

In *Admiralty* proceedings under s. 56 (1) of the Act, if the parties agree, by a memorandum signed by them or their solicitors or agents that a particular county court specified in the memorandum shall have jurisdiction, that court has power to hear and determine them (s. 56 (5)).

General

If proceedings have been commenced inadvertently in a county court which are beyond its jurisdiction, and this has not been discovered until the hearing, the action may proceed on the signing of an appropriate memorandum.

Where proceedings are commenced in a county court in which it has no jurisdiction, the court must, unless it is given jurisdiction by agreement, order the proceedings to be transferred to the High Court, but where, on the application of

B

any defendant, it appears to the court that the plaintiff or one of the plaintiffs knew or ought to have known that the court had no jurisdiction, the court may, instead of transferring the proceedings, order that they be struck out (s. 66).

In equity proceedings, if it appears that the subject matter exceeds the jurisdiction; or, on taking an account or making an inquiry, the registrar certifies that the subject matter exceeds the jurisdiction and the judge is of opinion that the excess exists; the judge must make an order to transfer the proceedings to the High Court if an appropriate agreement to jurisdiction is not signed, but the registrar may complete the account or inquiry (*Ord*. 16, *r*, 16).

Where the question of jurisdiction is one of venue alone, that is, when proceedings are commenced in the wrong county court, *Ord*. 16, *r*. 4, applies. Then in the absence of agreement, the court may either (*a*) transfer the proceedings to the correct court, or (*b*) order the proceedings to continue in the court in which they are commenced, or (*c*) order them to be struck out.

Other Statutes

County courts have jurisdiction under other statutes than the County Courts Act. These are dealt with under their respective headings.

COMMENCEMENT

Proceedings are commenced by
- (*a*) action;
- (*b*) originating application;
- (*c*) petition;
- (*d*) appeal;
- (*e*) some other proceeding specially provided for.

Venue

Order 2 sets out the general rules as to venue.

An *action* may be commenced, as a rule—
- (*a*) in the court for the district in which the defendant or one of the defendants resides or carries on business; or
- (*b*) in the court for the district in which the cause of action wholly or in part arose (*Ord*. 2, *r*. 1 (1)).

The price for goods sold is payable at the creditor's address in the absence of any agreement to the contrary. Default in payment is part of the cause of action. Therefore, non-payment as a cause of action would arise in the district of the county court in which the creditor's address is situated, unless payment was intended to be made elsewhere (*Northey Stone Co.* v. *Gidney* [1894] 1 Q.B. 99).

An *assignee* must sue in a court in which the assignor could have sued (*Ord. 2, r. 1 (2)*).

Where the defendant does not reside or carry on business in England or Wales and the claim is founded on tort, the action may be brought in the court for the district in which the plaintiff or one of the plaintiffs resides or carries on business (*Ord. 2, r. 1 (4)*).

In the case of an action arising out of (i) a *hire-purchase agreement* (but *not* claiming delivery of goods) or (ii) a contract for the sale or hire of goods under which the purchase price or rental is payable *otherwise than in one sum* (whether or not claiming delivery of goods), the action may be brought—

(*a*) in the court for the district in which the defendant or one of the defendants resides or carries on business; or

(*b*) in the court for the district in which the defendant or one of the defendants resided or carried on business when the contract was made (*Ord. 2, r, 1 (3)*).

The place of the cause of action does not determine the venue.

In the case of an action arising out of a *hire-purchase agreement* or a *conditional sale agreement*, to which the Hire-Purchase Act, 1965, applies, an action for the delivery of goods under s. 49 must be brought—

(*a*) in the court for the district in which the hirer or buyer resides or carries on business; or

(*b*) in the court for the district in which the hirer or buyer resided or carried on business at the date on which he last made a payment under the agreement (*ibid.*, s. 49).

In proceedings *against the Crown* the action must be commenced in the court for the district in which the cause of action wholly or in part arose, except where it is otherwise provided. If there is any reasonable doubt as to the court in which the action should be brought, it may be commenced in the court for the district in which the plaintiff or one of the plaintiffs resides or carries on business (*Ord*. 46, *r*. 13 (2)).

In claims for *possession of land*, and also in actions relating to *mortgages* or charges on land, whether for possession or for a money claim only, proceedings must be commenced in the court for the district in which the premises connected with the action are situated, but proceedings for enforcing a charging order on land under the County Courts Act, 1959, s. 141, must be commenced in the court where the charge was made (*Ord*. 2, *r*. 2).

Proceedings for enforcing a charge imposed on securities under *Ord*. 25, *r*. 6A, must be commenced in the court which imposed the charge (*Ord*. 2, *r*. 2A).

Proceedings under the *Settled Land Act*, 1925, must be commenced in the court for the district in which any part of the land connected with the subject matter is situated (*Ord*. 2, *r*. 3).

Proceedings under the *Trustee Act*, 1925, are commenced in the court for the district in which the persons or one of them making the application reside (*Ord*. 2, *r*. 4).

Proceedings for the *administration of the estate of a deceased person* are commenced in the court for the district in which the deceased person had his last place of residence in England and Wales, or where the executors or administrators or one of them reside (*Ord*. 2, *r*. 5).

Proceedings for the *dissolution or winding up of a partnership* are commenced in the court for the district in which the partnership business was or is carried on (*Ord*. 2, *r*. 6).

The venue in other proceedings is dealt with under the heading concerned.

Originating applications and petitions, subject to any act or rule, may be commenced:—

    (*a*) in the court for the district in which (i) the respondent or one of the respondents resides or carries on business; or (ii) the subject matter of the application is situated; or (*b*) if no respondent is named in the court for the district in which the applicant or petitioner or one of them resides or carries on business (*Ord.* 2, *rr.* 13 and 14).

In the case of an originating application against the Crown, the proceedings must be commenced in the court for the district in which the subject matter of the application is situated (*Ord.* 46, *r.* 13 (2)).

Appeals to county courts, subject to any Act or rule, are commenced in the court for the district in which the order, decision or award appealed against was made or given (*Ord.* 2, *r.* 15).

A *judge* or *registrar* may sue or be sued in accordance with the rules, but if the court in which the action would be commenced is a court of which he is judge or registrar, then the action may be commenced in the nearest court of which he is not the judge or registrar (*Ord.* 2, *r.* 12).

Actions

Actions are commenced by plaint, that is, by summons (*Ord.* 6, *r.* 1).

Requirements:—

(*a*) Form of request (referred to as *"præcipe"*) (see below);

(*b*) Particulars of claim and a copy for each defendant;

(*c*) Plaint fee; and fee for service by bailiff, where applicable (see table at Appendix III, *infra*);

(*d*) Stamped addressed envelope, if issued by post;

(*e*) If the address of the plaintiff is out of England and Wales, usually undertaking in *Form* 13 (not supplied by the court) in lieu of security under *Ord.* 3, *r.* 1;

(*f*) If plaintiff under disability, undertaking by next friend in *Form* 12 (supplied);

(*g*) Legal aid certificate, if any, and notice of certificate for service on the defendant (*Legal Aid* (*General*) *Regulations*, 1971, *reg.* 17 (3));

(*h*) If the summons is to be served by post, certificate in *Form* 6, which is printed on the reverse of most *præcipes*; in this case, there is no fee for service by the court and 25p is added to solicitor's costs on summons.

Forms of particulars of claim are supplied by the court to parties in person.

Plaint note is issued to the plaintiff, which gives a return day in the case of an ordinary summons, except in proceedings against the Crown (*Ord.* 46, *r.* 13 (4)) (and in Admiralty proceedings).

If service is to be *by solicitor or plaintiff*, this should be stated *clearly* on the *præcipe*. The summons is prepared by the court and affidavit of service (*Form* 35) is supplied on request. It should be noted that service on an individual in this case must be personal.

If service is to be effected *on a solicitor acting on behalf of the defendant*, this should be indicated *clearly* either by separate letter or below the defendant's name and address on the form of request or *præcipe*. No affidavit of service is required if the defendant's solicitor indorses acceptance of service and an address for service on the copy summons retained by the person effecting service (*Ord.* 8, *r.* 11). The indorsement must be dated, and the copy summons filed in court office.

"Præcipe" means a request for the issue of process or the doing of some other act by the registrar (*Ord.* 49, *r.* 2).

Forms of Request are supplied by court as follows:—

Ordinary summons in district, *Form* 7;

Ordinary summons in district, several actions, one plaintiff, *Form* 7 (several);

Additional request for summons for recovery of goods for service on representative, *Form* 7A;

Ordinary summons out of district, *Form* 8;

Summons for recovery of land, *Form* 9;

Additional request for summons for recovery of land for service on representative, *Form* 9A;

Default summons in district, *Form* 10;

Default summons in district, several actions, one plaintiff. *Form* 10 (several);

Default summons out of district, *Form* 11;

Admiralty action, *Form* 281.

Notes on the *præcipe* state the particulars required. The full Christian names of the plaintiff must be stated. The registered office of limited companies must be given and so described. A *præcipe* may be signed by the solicitor acting for the plaintiff.

Costs to be entered on the summons are given in Appendix I to this book.

Ordinary summons

An ordinary summons may not issue for a debt or liquidated demand unless it is within one of the exceptions, for which a default may not issue, e.g., a moneylender's claim (see *infra*), or unless it is a "Rent Action" (see *infra*) (*Ord. 6, r. 2*). If the action is for the purpose of approving an "infant's (or minor's) settlement", a date for hearing in chambers before a registrar is usually given. In such a case, the particulars of claim should contain a brief statement of the cause of action together with a request for the approval of the settlement or compromise (*Ord. 15, r. 19*). It is assumed that an ordinary summons would be issued even if the claim is for a liquidated demand.

A return day is fixed on the issue of an ordinary summons, except in proceedings against the Crown and in Admiralty proceedings. Except in an action for recovery of land, the return day must be a day fixed for the preliminary consideration on a pre-trial review under *Ord.* 21, unless the court otherwise directs (*Ord. 6, r. 3(3)*).

In some county courts a direction might be given that there be no pre-trial review in the case of moneylenders' claims and claims for return of goods on hire or hire-purchase. If, however, the return day is fixed for a pre-trial review and it transpires that no review is required, judgment may be entered on the return day (*Ord. 21, rr. 6, 7 and 8*).

An action by a mortgagee for possession of the mortgaged property may be heard in chambers (*Ord. 46, r. 21*).

Summonses are prepared by the court.

Forms of admission, defence and counterclaim are annexed by the court to the summons as appropriate.

Rent action (*Ord. 26, rr. 8 to 11*).

Where a landlord claims arrears of rent from a tenant or

former tenant who is still in occupation, the claim may be brought by a "rent action".

The action must be brought in the court for the district in which the land is situated. The request or *præcipe* must contain a statement that the plaintiff requires a summons in *Form* 410.

The summons with a copy of the particulars of claim attached must be served not less than seven clear days before the return day in accordance with *Ord*. 8, *r*. 39, that is, it may be served by prepaid post.

A form of admission, defence, etc., is not annexed to the summons. No provision is made for the filing of an admission or defence and a counterclaim may not be filed, since *Ord*. 9 does not apply (*Ord*. 26, *r*. 11(1)). However, the court may give directions under *Ord*. 13, *r*. 3, and may at any time direct that the proceedings continue as an ordinary action. If a pre-trial review is required, the registrar may send notice to the parties in *Form* 367 under *Ord*. 21, *r*. 10.

Default summons

An action to recover a debt or liquidated demand must be a default action except where it is brought—

(*a*) against a person under disability; or

(*b*) to recover money lent by a moneylender within the meaning of the Moneylenders Acts, 1900 to 1927, or for interest thereon, or to enforce any agreement or security in respect thereof; or

(*c*) to recover money secured by a mortgage or charge; or

(*d*) on a claim arising out of a hire-purchase agreement unless the claim is for no more than the amount of any instalment or instalments of the hire-purchase price which is or are due and unpaid; or

(*e*) to recover interest accruing after the commencement of the action (*Ord*. 6, *r*. 2); or

(*f*) against the Crown (*Ord*. 46, *r*. 13 (3)); or

(*g*) as an Admiralty action (*Ord*. 6, *r*. 2(3)).

No date of hearing is given on the issue of a default summons. The summons is in *Form* 22.

There is no satisfactorily authoritative definition of a liquidated demand and county courts differ in border-line cases. The original term was "debt or liquidated demand in money arising upon a contract" (see Common Law Procedure Act, 1852, s. 25). For liquidated damages to be a liquidated demand, it is suggested that they should be the subject of an agreement, which, in the case of tort, supersedes the original cause of action. In doubtful cases, the matter is referred to the registrar for his personal decision. A claim of *quantum meruit* is treated as a liquidated demand.

A claim for the cost of repairs executed to a vehicle in consequence of damage, sustained in an accident on land, due to the defendant's negligence is treated as a liquidated demand unless the court otherwise orders (*Ord.* 49, *r.* 5(1)). A claim for damages for the loss of use of a vehicle pending its repair is also treated as a liquidated demand but not for the purposes of issuing a default action (*Ord.* 49, *r.* 5).

Matters

Originating applications (Ord. 6, r. 4)

Requirements on issue:

(a) Originating application (*Form* 23) with a copy for each respondent to be served.

(b) Fee for issue and for service by bailiff where appropriate (see table in Appendix III, *infra*) ;

(c) Stamped addressed envelope, if issued by post ;

(d) If address of applicant or petitioner out of England and Wales, usually undertaking in *Form* 13 (not supplied) in lieu of security under *Ord.* 3, *r.* 1 ;

(e) If applicant under disability, undertaking by next friend in *Form* 12 (supplied) ;

(f) Legal aid certificate, if any, and notice of certificate for service on respondent.

Summary proceedings for recovery of land (Ord. 26, rr. 1 to 7).

Where a person claims possession of land which he alleges is occupied solely by a person or persons (not being a tenant or tenants holding over) who are in occupation without his licence or consent or that of his predecessor the proceedings may be brought by originating application.

Requirements:-

(a) Originating application in *Form* 398 and copy for each respondent;

(b) Affidavit in support with copies for service;

(c) *Fee* (No. 2(iv)), £3, and for service by bailiff, 50p.

For contents of affidavit, see *Ord.* 26, *r.* 2.

The court prepares notice of hearing in *Form* 26; where the applicant is unable, after taking reasonable steps, to identify every person occupying the land to make him a respondent, the conclusion of *Form* 26 is in *Form* 399.

Service is effected in accordance with *Ord.* 26, *r.* 3, not less than seven clear days before hearing.

An order for possession must be made by a judge and is in *Form* 400.

Petitions (Ord. 6, r. 5)

Requirements on issue :

(a) Petition (*Form* 24) with a copy for each respondent to be served ;

(b) Fee for issue and service (see table in Appendix III, *infra*). Then as for originating application.

Originating applications and petitions-general

A *præcipe* is not required for originating applications and petitions.

Plaint note is issued to the applicant or petitioner which states date of hearing.

Forms 23 and 24, originating application and petition, are not supplied by the court. In some proceedings special forms are prescribed and dealt with under the respective headings.

The forms of application and petition, *Forms* 23 and 24, commence with "I" followed by the full name of the applicant or petitioner. They may, however, be accepted if signed by the solicitor for and on behalf of his client.

A notice in *Form* 26, instead of a summons, giving the date of hearing, is prepared by the court for service on the respondent and a copy of the originating application or petition is annexed to the notice to be served. In certain proceedings, other forms are prescribed, as for instance, in legitimacy proceedings (*Form* 324) and in adoption proceedings.

Appeals to County Courts (Ord. 6, r. 6)
Requirements on issue:—

    (*a*) Request for entry of appeal (*Form* 25, unless otherwise prescribed) and copy for each respondent to be served;

    (*b*) A copy of the order or decision or award appealed against;

    (*c*) Where the enactment under which the appeal lies requires the appellant to give to the other parties notice in writing of his intention to appeal and of the grounds of his appeal, a copy of such notice, and in any other case he must include in the request a statement of the grounds of the appeal;

    (*d*) Fees £1.50 (No. 3) and for service by bailiff 50p;

    (*e*) Other papers and documents, as in an originating application.

The appeal must be filed within twenty-one days after the date of the order, decision or award appealed from, in the absence of any provision to the contrary.

The procedure follows that of originating applications.

It should be noted that the request for an entry of an appeal is not in the nature of a *"præcipe"* but takes the place of a pleading.

Proceedings in wrong form
If proceedings are commenced by action, which should have been commenced by originating application, or *vice versa*, the judge may allow or order them to continue in the one form or the other (*Ord.* 6, *r.* 7).

Where proceedings which ought to have been brought by ordinary action are brought by default action, and *vice versa*, the court may either strike out the proceedings or order them to continue in accordance with the procedure for an ordinary action (*Ord.* 6, *r.* 7(3)).

PARTICULARS OF CLAIM

General

Order 7 deals with particulars of claim and *Ord.* 4 with joinder of causes of action.

Forms of particulars of claim are supplied by the court to parties in person.

Claims by plaintiffs jointly may be joined with claims by them or any of them separately against the same defendant (*Ord.* 4, *r.* 1(*c*)). The total claim may not exceed the jurisdiction. This seems to follow from the Act, but there appears to be no authority directly on the point.

No cause of action may be joined with an action for the recovery of land, unless leave is given, except claims for mesne profits or arrears of rent or for damages for breach of any contract under which the land is held or for any wrong or injury to it, or for payment of money or interest secured by a mortgage or charge (*Ord.* 4, *r.* 2(*c*)).

Particulars of claim must be signed by the solicitor (if any) acting for the plaintiff (*Ord.* 7, *r.* 10). The following wording may be used:—

"*A.B.* & Co.

of   [address], Solicitors for the Plaintiff, who at this address will accept service of all documents on his behalf."

The signature should be legible or repeated in type because it is from this signature that notices and orders are addressed. A signature by a facsimile stamp is sufficient but a normal signature in ink avoids queries. It is not necessary for a plaintiff in person to sign his particulars of claim although it is desirable that he does so.

If settled by counsel, the particulars of claim should show his name in capital letters as having signed them.

In the case of ordinary debts, such as for goods sold or work done, the form of the plaintiff's bill or account is usually accepted, but they should show the consideration, "goods sold," "work done and materials supplied," etc. "Account *rendered*" is not sufficient. "Account stated" is an accepted cause of action recognised in law. The date of the cause of action should be indicated. Insufficient particulars may cause payment of costs.

If a plaintiff abandons the excess of his claim over £750 to bring it within the jurisdiction of the county court, the abandonment must be stated at the end of the particulars (*Ord. 7, r.* 1(2)). Particulars of claim and the *præcipe* do not have to indicate that a claim is limited to £750, but a statement that the claim is so limited is best added. However, where a plaintiff in the first instance desires to have an *account* taken, the particulars must state the amount which the plaintiff claims subject to it, and if no amount is stated, the plaintiff will be deemed to claim £750 (*Ord. 7, r.* 2).

Recovery of Land

In an action for recovery of land, the particulars must state:
  (*a*) full description of the land;
  (*b*) net annual value of it for rating, or, if the land does not have a separate net annual value for rating, then (i) where the land forms part of a hereditament having a net annual value not exceeding the county court limit, that is, £1,000, the net annual value of that hereditament, or (ii) in any other case, the value of the land by the year;
  (*c*) the rent, if any, of the land; and
  (*d*) the ground on which possession is claimed (*Ord. 7, r.* 3).

The *præcipe* indicates what is required.

Administration proceedings and for execution of a trust

For administration proceedings and proceedings for the execution of a trust, the particulars required are set out in *Ord. 7, r.* 5.

Moneylenders' actions

In moneylenders' actions, the particulars must state that the plaintiff, or the assignor, if an assignee sues, was a licensed moneylender at the time of making the loan or contract, and must include:

(i) the date on which the loan was made;

(ii) the amount actually lent to the borrower;

(iii) the rate per cent. per annum of interest charged;

(iv) the date of the note or memorandum in writing of the contract;

(v) the date when the contract was signed by the borrower;

(vi) the date when a copy of the contract was delivered or sent to the borrower;

(vii) the amount of every payment already received by the moneylender in respect of the loan and the date on which it was made;

(viii) the amount of every sum due to the moneylender but unpaid;

(ix) the date upon which every such sum became due;

(x) the amount of interest accrued due and unpaid on every such sum (*Ord.* 7, *r.* 6).

Interest is said to be unconscionable under the Moneylenders Act, 1927, s. 10, if it exceeds 48% per annum.

Mortgage actions

In mortgage actions, where the plaintiff claims principal money or interest, the particulars must state:

(i) the date of the mortgage or charge;

(ii) the amount of the principal money lent;

(iii) the amount remaining due and unpaid in respect of (*a*) principal and (*b*) interest;

(iv) what proceedings (if any) the plaintiff has taken against the defendant in respect of the property mortgaged or charged, and whether he has obtained possession of it (*Ord.* 7, *r.* 7(1)).

Where the plaintiff claims possession of the property mortgaged or charged, the particulars must state:

(i) the date of the mortgage or charge;

(ii) whether or not the property consists of or includes a dwelling-house within the meaning of Pt. IV of the Administration of Justice Act, 1970;

(iii) the state of the account between the plaintiff and
defendant with details of:—
    (*a*) the amount of the advance;
    (*b*) the sums payable from time to time under or
    in connection with mortgage or charge;
    (*c*) the amount of any such sums in arrear;
    (*d*) the amount remaining due under the mortgage
    of charge;
(iv) what proceedings (if any) the plaintiff has taken
against the defendant in respect of the principal
money or interest (*Ord.* 7, *r.* 7(2)).

A dwelling-house within the meaning of Pt. IV of the Administration of Justice Act, 1970, includes any building or
part thereof which is used as a dwelling. The fact that part of
the premises comprised in a dwelling-house is used as a shop
or for business, trade or profession purposes does not prevent
it being a dwelling-house (*ibid.*, s. 39).

Hire-purchase actions

In *hire purchase* cases, where a plaintiff claims the delivery
of goods let under a hire purchase agreement to a person other
than a body corporate, he must state in the particulars in the
order following:—
    (i) date of the agreement and the parties thereto;
    (ii) place where the agreement was signed by the hirer;
    (iii) goods claimed;
    (iv) amount of the hire purchase price;
    (v) amount paid by or on behalf of the hirer;
    (vi) amount of the unpaid balance of the hire purchase
    price;
    (vii) whether a notice of default within the meaning of
    the Hire-Purchase Act, 1965, s. 25, has been served
    on the hirer, and if it has, the date on which it was
    so served;
    (viii) date when the right to demand delivery of the goods
    accrued;
    (ix) amount, if any, claimed as an alternative to the
    delivery of the goods; and

(x) amounts, if any, claimed in addition to the delivery
of the goods or any claim under sub-para. (ix),
stating the cause of action in respect of which each
claim is made (*Ord. 7, r.* 7A (1)).

Where a plaintiff's claim arises out of a hire-purchase agreement but is not for the delivery of goods, he must state in the
particulars in the order following:—

(i) date of the agreement and the parties thereto;
(ii) the goods let under the agreement;
(iii) the amount of the hire-purchase price;
(iv) the amount paid by or on behalf of the hirer;
(v) the amount, if any, claimed as being due and unpaid
in respect of any instalment or instalments of the
hire-purchase price;
(vi) the amount of any other claim and the circumstances
in which it arises (*Ord. 7, r.* 7A (2)).

PARTIES

Plaintiff residing out of England and Wales.—In this case, the
general rule is that security for costs must be given (*Ord. 3,
r.* 1 (1)). On an *ex parte* application by the plaintiff, the
registrar may dispense with security (*Ord. 3, r.* 1 (2)). This
procedure is unusual. In practice, the registrar accepts an
undertaking by a solicitor in *Form* 13 (*Ord. 48, r.* 16) without
application being made. The form is not supplied.

A corporation resides where it carries on business and it
can reside in more places than one (*Davies* v. *British Geon, Ltd.*
[1956] 3 All E.R. 389). Therefore, if a plaintiff limited company
can give a place of business within England and Wales,
security or an undertaking is not required.

Assignees.—Plaintiff's name is given as: "A.B. [address and
description] assignee of X. Y. [address and description]."

Charitable institutions.—See note 65/3/2 to R.S.C., *Ord.* 65,
r. 3, in *Supreme Court Practice.*

Club.—A proprietary club sues, or is sued, in its corporate
name, if it is a limited company, or, if not corporate, then in

the same way as a firm. In a members' club, it is usual to allow one or more of the members (usually, two or three prominent members) to sue or be sued "on their own behalf and on behalf of all other members of the . . . Club" if they have a common interest with all the other members.

Limited company.—The registered office must be given. No other address need be stated on the *præcipe* unless it is for the purpose of showing an address within England and Wales, or to show to what address notices for a plaintiff company should be sent. The head office is not necessarily the registered office. A limited company may sue and act without a solicitor in county courts and is usually allowed to do so and to appear in court without a solicitor, except, very often, in a defended action for hearing before a judge. Note *Kinnel & Co., Ltd.* v. *Harding, Wace & Co.* [1918] 1 K.B. 155 and 405.

Company in liquidation.—The words "(in liquidation)" should follow the name, and after the address, there should be added: "by the liquidator A.B. of [address and description].'

Crown.—The title of the department suing or being sued must be precisely stated in accordance with the list of Crown Departments published under the Crown Proceedings Act, 1947, s. 17. A list appears in the *County Court Practice* after *Ord.* 46, *r.* 13 (in the 1973 edition on p. 1260). When the Crown is being sued, reference should be made to *Ord.* 46, *r.* 13. A default action and a rent action may not be brought against the Crown. A summons is not served in the first instance but a notice in *Form* 25A to which is annexed the particulars of claim. If, within twenty-eight days of service, the Crown does not file two copies of a demand for further information, the registrar then fixes a day for hearing and the summons is served. Modifications as to practice, and venue, are contained in *Ord.* 46, *r.* 13.

Firm.—Two or more persons carrying on business within England and Wales may sue and be sued in the name of the firm in which they were partners when the cause of action arose (*Ord.* 5, *r.* 21 (1)). The words "(suing as a firm)" or "(sued as a firm)," as the case may be, must follow the firm name. A person carrying on business in a name other than his own may *be sued* in the firm name, but he may not sue in the firm name. When the owner or partners of a business are suing or being sued as individuals then the words "trading as [*or*, practising as, *or*, *as the case may be*] X. Y. and Co." follow the names.

Person under disability.—Such a person for the purpose of the rules is defined as a person who is a *minor* or *mental patient.* A mental patient means a person who, by reason of mental disorder within the meaning of the Mental Health Act, 1959, is incapable of managing and administering his property and affairs (*Ord.* 49, *r.* 2). A minor or mental patient must sue by his next friend, except that a minor may sue in a county court for wages and piece work as if he were an adult without a next friend (*Ord.* 5, *r.* 11, and s. 80 of the Act). The plaintiff's name appears as "*A. B.* (a minor) suing by *C. B.* (his [father and] next friend)". An undertaking by the next friend in *Form* 12 must be filed (*Ord.* 3, *r.* 2). This form is supplied. Where proceedings have begun without a next friend the court may either, on the application of a party, appoint a person to act as a next friend who consents to act and gives an undertaking in *Form* 12, or order the proceedings to be struck out (*Ord.* 3, *r.* 4).

A person under disability may not defend except by his guardian *ad litem* (*Ord.* 5, *r.* 11). The defendant's name appears as "*A. B.* (a minor) by *C. B.* (his guardian *ad litem*)."

Where it appears *on the face of the proceedings* that a defendant is a person under disability, *Ord.* 5, *r.* 13, applies. At any time after service of the summons, and not less than six days before the return day, an application may be made to the registrar on behalf of the person under disability for the appointment of a guardian *ad litem.*

Requirements:

(*a*) affidavit in *Form* 45, the consent of the proposed guardian *ad litem* appearing at the foot of the form;

(*b*) in the case of a mental patient, an office copy of an order or other authorisation, if any, under Pt. VIII of the Mental Health Act, 1959.

No fee.

Form 45 is not supplied by the court. The affidavit would be made by the solicitor acting for the defendant.

An order is in *Form* 46, and the court sends notice to the plaintiff in *Form* 47.

Where no application is made for the appointment of a guardian *ad litem*, the court must send notice to the plaintiff in *Form* 48 on the sixth day before the return day. The plaintiff must apply to the judge for an order for the appointment of a guardian *ad litem* before taking any further step in the proceedings (*Ord*. 5, *r*. 13 (*c*)).

Requirements:

(*a*) notice of application in *Form* 49 and copy;

(*b*) affidavit in *Form* 50 and copy, the consent of the proposed guardian *ad litem* appearing at the foot of the form.

No fee.

Forms are not supplied by the court.

Arrangements are made to adjourn the hearing of the action pending the hearing of the application.

The plaintiff serves the copy notice and copy affidavit. Service must be effected on the person on whom the summons was required to be served not less than three clear days before the hearing of the application. Service may be by post.

On the hearing of the application, the judge may appoint the person proposed by the plaintiff, or, if not satisfied that the person proposed is a proper person to be appointed, may appoint any other person willing to act, or in default of any such person, may appoint the registrar. As a rule, it is not practicable to appoint the registrar, and if a proper person cannot be found, consideration should be given to the appointment of the Official Solicitor. If a registrar is appointed, it may be necessary to transfer the action to a court of which he is not the registrar. The order to appoint a guardian *ad litem* is in *Form* 51.

NOTE: Where a minor is sued for a liquidated demand, *Form* 48 is not sent and an application does not have to be made unless the court otherwise orders (*Ord*. 5, *r*. 13).

Where it *does not appear on the face of the proceedings*, but appears in the course of them that any defendant is a person under disability, *Ord*. 5, *r*. 14 applies.

If, on a defendant appearing on the return day, it appears that he is a *minor*, and he names a person as guardian who consents to act, that person must be appointed guardian. If the defendant does not name a guardian, the judge may appoint any person present who is willing to act, or, if there is no such person, the judge may appoint the registrar. This does not apply to a person who is a mental patient. The order is in *Form* 52 or 53.

In any other case where it appears that any defendant is under disability, an application may be made to appoint a guardian *ad litem* within six days of its appearing that a defendant is a person under disability in the same way as if it appeared on the face of the proceedings that the defendant was under disability. If no application is made within the six days, the court must send a notice in *Form* 48 to the plaintiff and the plaintiff must apply to the judge in *Form* 49 supported by an affidavit in *Form* 50, as above.

NOTE: Where a minor is sued for a liquidated demand, the above does not apply unless the court otherwise orders (*Ord*. 5, *r*. 14).

If judgment has been obtained without the appointment of a guardian *ad litem*, *Ord*. 5, *rr*. 17 and 18, apply and the judge may set the judgment or order aside.

Where money is claimed or recovered on behalf of a person under disability, no settlement or compromise or acceptance of money in court is valid without the sanction of the judge or registrar, except where a minor sues for wages under s. 80 of the Act. (*Ord*. 5, *r*. 19).

Trustees, executors and administrators (Ord. 5, r. 7).—Their names, addresses and descriptions should be given in full followed by the description of their capacity with regard to the estate, such as, "Executors of *A. B.* deceased." The Proceedings against Estates Act, 1970, allows proceedings to be brought against the estate of a deceased person before there

has been a grant of probate or administration. The action is
brought against "the personal representatives of *A. B.*
deceased." *Order* 5, *r.* 34A, applies.

Trustee in bankruptcy should sue (or be sued) in his official
title, "Trustee of the property of *A. B.* a bankrupt" without
adding his own name (Bankruptcy Act, 1914, s. 76, and
Pooley's Trustee v. *Whetham* (1884), 28 Ch. D. 38).

Other parties.—*See County Court Practice*, particularly the
notes after *Ord.* 5, *r.* 1, and also the *Supreme Court Practice.*

SERVICE

Generally

Order 8 applies to service.

Where *personal service* of a document is required, a bailiff
may serve it, and, if the place of service is not within the
district of the court of which he is bailiff, the document will
be sent to the appropriate court for service. The bailiff
endorses on the copy of the document a note of the manner
and date of service. If the bailiff fails to effect service, notice
of non-service is sent by the court of which he is bailiff to
the plaintiff or other party issuing the process. *Fee:* for each
person to be served 50p, except a jury summons, an order
in *Form* 179, an interpleader summons under execution, and
an originating application for an adoption order or under the
Rent (County Court Proceedings) Rules, 1970; or for service
on a limited company which is by post. If the document is
amended after delivery to the bailiff, a *fee* of 25p is payable.

Where a party or his solicitor serves, service is proved by
affidavit. The affidavit of service in *Form* 35 (general form)
or 177 (judgment summons) should be filed within three days.
Affidavit of service of a witness summons is in *Form* 116 (2) and
need not be filed unless enforcement of it is required. These
forms are supplied by the court.

Substituted service is now unusual. *Ord.* 8, *r.* 6, applies.

No process (except a summons *in rem* or a warrant of arrest
in an Admiralty action) may be served or executed within
England or Wales on a Sunday, Christmas Day or Good Friday
except, in case of urgency, with the leave of the court. (*Ord.* 8,
r. 3).

Ordinary Summons and Default Summons

An ordinary summons must be served not less than twenty-one clear days before the return day, but it may be served at any time before the return day on the plaintiff satisfying the registrar by affidavit that a defendant is about to remove (*Ord.* 8, *r.* 8(4)).

Service of a summons is usually effected by the court. If the address for service is not within the district of the court issuing it, and it is not to be served by post, the summons is sent for service to the court within the district of which the address for service is situated. (*Ord.* 8, *r.* 7).

If the plaintiff or his solicitor wishes to serve the summons, it will be handed or sent to him. Form of affidavit of service (*Form* 35) is supplied on request. In this case, service on an individual defendant must be personal, unless a solicitor accepts service on his behalf. The rule that an affidavit of service must be filed within three days of service is directory and not mandatory. It is not always enforced for practical reasons. However, until it is filed, judgment will not be entered and the action will not be included in the list for hearing.

An ordinary or default summons may be served by delivering the summons to an individual defendant *personally*, or, if *by a bailiff*, to a person apparently not less than sixteen years of age at the defendant's residence, or, if the defendant is a proprietor of a business, at his place of business (*Ord.* 8, *r.* 8 (1)).

The court may serve an *ordinary or default summons by post*, if the plaintiff or his solicitor gives a certificate in *Form* 6, which is printed on *præcipes* supplied by the court (*Ord.* 8, *r.* 8 (2)).

Where a summons does not come to the knowledge of a defendant, see *Supreme Court Practice*, para. 65/5/3.

Where it appears to a bailiff that there is a reasonable probability that the summons would come to the knowledge of the defendant in due time if it were delivered at the address stated in the *præcipe*, the summons may be served by:—

(*a*) an officer of the court sending the summons by ordinary post to the defendant at that address; or

(*b*) the bailiff inserting the summons, enclosed in an envelope addressed to the defendant, in the letter-box at that address;

with the general or special leave of the registrar (*Ord.* 8, *r.* 8(3)). It is usual for a registrar to give general leave. The rule refers to the address in the *præcipe*. It is a matter of opinion whether *Ord.* 8, *r.* 29(*a*) allows service at an address other than that stated in the *præcipe* without amendment.

Notice of service in *Form* 38 is sent to the plaintiff when a default summons is served by the court (*Ord.* 8, *r.* 33).

On solicitor for defendant.—The solicitor endorses on the copy summons retained by the person effecting service, a memorandum that he accepts service and giving an address for service (*Ord.* 8, *r.* 11). No affidavit of service is required. The indorsement must be dated. The copy summons must be filed.

Crown and Government Department.—Reference should be made to *Ord.* 46, *r.* 13.

Minor and mental patient (*Ord.* 8, *r.* 13).—If a defendant is a minor, an ordinary summons must be served, if he is not a mental patient, on his father or guardian, or, if he has no father or guardian, then on the person with whom he resides or in whose care he is. If the father has left the home, in practice service is effected as if he had no father. If the defendant is a mental patient, the summons must be served on the person (if any) who is authorised under the Mental Health Act, 1959, Pt. VIII, to conduct proceedings on the defendant's behalf, or, if there is no such person, then on the person with whom he resides or in whose care he is. Even if a summons is served on a person under disability otherwise than above, the court may order that the summons be duly served. A default summons may not be issued against a person under disability. A guardian *ad litem* is not appointed until after service.

Firm (*Ord.* 8, *r.* 14).—Where a defendant is sued as if a firm, the summons may be served on a partner personally, or the person carrying on business in the firm name, or at the principal place of business of the firm within the district of the court by delivering it to the person having, or appearing to have, control or management there. If the firm has been dissolved to the knowledge of the plaintiff before the commencement of the action, the summons must be served on every person in England and Wales sought to be made liable.

Limited company.—A summons may be served on a limited company by leaving it at, or by sending it by post to, the registered office (Companies Act, 1948, s. 437 (1)). It is advisable to serve by ordinary post: see *T. O. Supplies (London), Ltd.* v. *Jerry Creighton, Ltd.* [1951] 2 All E.R. 992. For Scottish companies, see under "Service out of England and Wales," *infra*.

Corporation aggregate (Ord. 8, *r.* 26).—Service may be effected on the mayor or other head officer, or on the town clerk, clerk, treasurer or secretary, in the absence of any statutory provision.

Recovery of land or goods (Ord. 8, *r.* 24).—If a summons for recovery of land or goods cannot be effectively served in the usual manner, it may be served *on a representative*, in which case a notice in *Form* 389 is annexed to the summons. The plaintiff must first file an additional *præcipe* in *Form* 7A (goods) or 9A (land). The meaning of "representative" is set out in this rule, and means, *inter alia*, the wife or husband of the defendant.

In an action for recovery of land, in the case of *vacant possession* or where the property is occupied only by virtue of the presence of furniture or other goods, the summons may be served on a representative of the defendant and also by affixing it to a conspicuous part of the property or in either manner (*Ord.* 8, *r.* 24 (3)).

If the summons for recovery of land or goods has been served only in the above manner, the court may mark it "not served." if it thinks it just, and, if a money claim is joined, it must, in the absence of special circumstances, mark the summons "not served" as to the money claim but may proceed to hear the claim for recovery of the land or goods, but the court may suspend a judgment conditionally on payment of money and may make an order for costs (*Ord.* 8, *r.* 24 (10)).

Other modes of service and service on other persons.— See the *County Court Practice* and also the *Supreme Court Practice.*

Doubtful service.—If it is doubtful from the indorsement whether the summons will come to the knowledge of the defendant in sufficient time, notice of doubtful service is sent by the court in *Form* 37 (ordinary summons) or *Form* 39 (default summons) (*Ord.* 8, *rr.* 30 and 31). Where a summons has been served in accordance with the usual rules as to service, but the court receives from the defendant a defence, admission or counterclaim, the action may proceed as if the summons has been duly served. (*Ord.* 8, *r.* 12).

Non-service.—If the court is unable to effect service, notice of non-service in *Form* 36 is sent to the plaintiff or his solicitor. In the case of default summonses, the bailiff must make a return after one month from issue, and after every subsequent month until a final return is made (*Ord.* 8, *rr.* 28 and 34). Notice of service is sent only in the case of default summonses.

Error in præcipe (*Ord.* 8, *r.* 29).—If a summons has not been served, it may be amended if the plaintiff files an amended *præcipe*, "notwithstanding that the amendment consists of the substitution of a defendant."

Requirements:

    (*a*) amended *præcipe* (out of district, if necessary);

    (*b*) plaint note;

    (*c*) *fees:* on filing *præcipe*, 15p, and, in addition if service by bailiff but not by post, 25p;

    (*d*) stamped addressed envelope, if requested by post.

If the bailiff knows or ascertains, before notice of non-service is sent, that the defendant is at another address within the district, he should attempt to serve the summons there (*Ord.* 8, *r.* 29 (*a*)).

If, on amendment, it is found that the court does not have jurisdiction by virtue of the change in address, an application can be made to transfer it to the appropriate court under

Ord. 16, *r.* 4. *Fees:* 50p; certificate of order, 5p. Courts will, however, entertain an application by letter, setting out the facts, for the return of the plaint fee so that the action may be re-commenced in the correct court. This course would not be advisable where time under the Statutes of Limitation has expired.

For amendment generally, *Ord.* 15 applies; see *infra*.

Successive summons (*Ord.* 8, *r.* 32).—Where an ordinary summons has not been served on any defendant before the return day, the summons may be re-issued against the defendant not served for another return day, and the summons is called a successive summons.

Requirements:

    (*a*) fresh or amended *præcipe*—letter is accepted;

    (*b*) plaint note—to mark fee and new hearing;

    (*c*) no fee on first successive summons unless error in *præcipe*, then 15p for filing an amended *præcipe* and 25p for service. For second and every subsequent summons, 50p.

A successive summons must be issued within twelve months from the date of the issue of the original summons. A summons or successive summons may be amended after that period provided a fresh return day does not have to be given. The alteration of the return day is the criterion which determines whether it is a successive (or further successive) summons.

However, the registrar may extend the period for a further period not exceeding twelve months, and successive periods, if reasonable efforts have been made to serve the summons provided that the application is made before the summons expires. The application, setting out the facts, may be made on *Form* Ex. 23, but most courts accept a letter. It is made *ex parte* and usually without attendance. No fee. A note of the extension is made by the court on the summons and copy and a new plaint number is given. The plaint note should be produced.

Extension of default summons (*Ord.* 8, *r.* 35).—A default summons must be served within twelve months from the date of issue. The registrar may extend the time for service for a period not exceeding twelve months and for successive periods, where reasonable efforts have been made to serve the summons. The application must be made during the currency of the summons.

The application, setting out the facts, may be made on *Form* Ex. 23, but most courts accept a letter. It is made *ex parte* and usually without attendance. No fee. A note of the extension is made by the court on the summons and copy and a new plaint number is given. The plaint note should be produced.

When a default summons has expired, it is struck out (*Ord.* 8, *r.* 35 (4)). The better opinion seems to be that the time for service may not be extended after the summons has been struck out.

Service of Matters

Service of an originating application, petition or appeal to county court, with *Form* 26, is in accordance with the rules for an ordinary summons unless any enactment or rule provides otherwise (*Ord.* 6, *rr.* 4, 5 and 6).

Where, in the case of an ordinary summons, an amended *præcipe* would be required, the rules require that an amended originating application, petition or request for appeal be filed (*Ord.* 6, *r.* 4 (2) (*e*)). If the amendment is trifling or short, and the document to be amended is a long one, the amendment is usually made by the court following a request in that behalf by letter. Fees payable are similar to those for an ordinary summons.

NOTE.—Originating applications under the Landlord and Tenant Act, 1954, s. 24 (for a new tenancy), must be served within one month of issue unless the period is extended before it expires (*Ord.* 40, *r.* 8 (1A)).

Other documents

Order 8, *r.* 39, applies to the service of other documents. Where in any proceedings in a county court any document is required to be served on a person and no other mode of service is prescribed, the document may be served as for personal service or it may be sent by prepaid post to his residence or last known residence or delivered there; or in the case of a proprietor of a business, to his last known place of business. Where a person to be served is acting by solicitors service may be made on the solicitor.

Service out of England and Wales (*Ord.* 8, *rr.* 40 *to* 50)

When a defendant has no address for service in England and Wales, application may be made to serve out of England and Wales where conditions set out in *Ord.* 8, *rr.* 41 and 41A, apply. Application may be made before the issue of the proceedings.

Requirements:

(*a*) *Form* Ex. 23 or letter—not always required;

(*b*) affidavit in support;

(*c*) copy of the proposed particulars of claim—not necessary, but useful;

(*d*) *fee:* 50p.

The application is made to the judge. A plaint number and plaint note are not given at this stage.

It is not usual for an appointment to be given in the first place unless the judge requires the attendance of the applicant or his solicitor. If attendance is required, the application is heard in chambers.

The affidavit must give particulars required by *Ord.* 8, *r.* 44. The grounds on which the application is made should follow the conditions set out in one of the paragraphs of *Ord.* 8, *r.* 41, or, in the case of an Admiralty action under s. 70 of the Act which relates to collision and similar cases, the conditions set out in *Ord.* 8, *r.* 41A. The order is in *Form* 42.

This procedure does not apply to proceedings against the Crown (*Ord.* 46, *r.* 13 (6)).

All types of originating process, including a third party notice, may be served abroad (*Ord.* 8, *r.* 40). *Quaere*, whether an Admiralty summons *in rem* may be served abroad—in the High Court a writ *in rem* may not be.

As to the service of interlocutory process out of England and Wales, see *Ord.* 8, *r.* 42.

When giving leave, the judge must fix the return day, or, in the case of a default summons, the time for delivering an admission or paying the total claim and costs (*Ord.* 8, *r.* 45). The time can be fixed by reference to the Extra Jurisdiction Tables in the *Supreme Court Practice*, Vol. 2, para. 941.

Where leave is asked for service in Scotland or in Northern Ireland, the judge must have regard to the comparative cost and convenience and to the powers of the sheriffs' courts in Scotland and the county courts in Northern Ireland (*Ord.* 8, *r.* 43).

A limited company with a registered office in Scotland and carrying on business in England and Wales can be served without leave. Service is effected by serving by post or delivering the process at the address in England and Wales and at the same time sending a copy of the process to the registered office (Companies Act, 1948, s. 437 (2) and (3)).

As to modes of service, see *Ord.* 8, *rr.* 46, 47 and 48. *Præcipe* for service through the court (*Form* 44) is supplied. Service through the court is limited to service in a convention country or any other country not mentioned in *Ord.* 8, *r.* 46 (6). The *County Court Practice* must be referred to.

PAYMENT INTO COURT BEFORE JUDGMENT
(*Ord.* 11)

Money may be paid into court at any time before judgment (*Ord.* 11, *r.* 1).

Requirements:

  (*a*) cash, or if by post, postal order; cheques from solicitors are usually accepted, and from reputable companies; bankers' drafts are accepted;

  (*b*) summons or originating process;

  (*c*) stamped addressed envelope, if by post;

  (*d*) if not full payment of claim and costs where money claim only, notice (or letter) to say how payment made, e.g., in satisfaction, on account, etc. No form prescribed. If more than one defendant, notice or letter, to say by which defendant paid.

Postal orders, cheques and bankers' drafts should be made payable to H.M. Paymaster-General.

A receipt is given by the court official on an official form. Notice of payment into court is drawn and sent by the court to the plaintiff or his solicitor, and to any defendant who has not joined in the payment. *Forms* 64, 65, 66 and 69 (*Ord.* 11, *r.* 6).

Claim for money only, payment of whole claim

If payment is made in full with costs on summons within fourteen days of service (inclusive of day of service) and the plaintiff is not under disability the action is stayed (*Ord.* 11, *r.* 7 (1)). The defendant is not liable for further costs (*a*) in the case of a liquidated demand, unless the court otherwise orders —such orders are rare, (*b*) in any other case, unless, within seven days after the receipt of notice of payment but not less than two days before the return day, the plaintiff sends to the registrar and every defendant notice that he requires his costs to be taxed (*Ord.* 11, *r.* 7 (3A)).

If the costs on the summons are not paid, the plaintiff then proceeds to judgment for them. In the case of a default summons, he may enter judgment in default.

If the whole money claim and costs are paid, but *not within fourteen days* of service, the action is stayed and the defendant is not liable for any costs incurred *after* the receipt by the plaintiff of the notice of payment. Whether or not the claim is for a liquidated demand, if the plaintiff claims additional costs to the costs on the summons, he may within fourteen days of the receipt of the notice lodge a bill of costs for taxation. If the costs are not paid within fourteen days after taxation, he may enter judgment for them, usually on filing a letter requesting judgment. (*Ord.* 11, *r.* 8).

Payment of part of claim, where claim for money only

The payment of part of a claim is deemed to be on account unless accompanied by a notice indicating the contrary (*Ord.* 11, *r.* 2).

Where payment into court is made in satisfaction of a

claim or of one of several causes of action, the accompanying notice must state that the money is paid in satisfaction of all the causes of action or of such of the causes of action as may be specified in the notice, and must specify the sum paid in satisfaction of any cause or causes of action in respect of which the defendant desires to make a separate payment (*Ord.* 11, *rr.* 2 and 3). This notice must not be with the pleadings or documents before the court at the trial until after its decision, except in the case of a defence of tender or the filing of a plea under the Libel Acts (*Ord.* 11, *r.* 15).

Notice to the plaintiff of payment into court is in *Form* 65, or, if payment is on account, *Form* 69; notice to a joint defendant is in *Form* 66. Notices are drawn and sent by the court.

If (*a*) the claim is for money only, and (*b*) the plaintiff is not under disability, and (*c*) the defendant pays money into court in satisfaction within fourteen days of service, and (*d*) he pays into court at the same time the appropriate costs which would be entered on a summons, he will not be liable for further costs where the plaintiff accepts the amount in satisfaction *unless* (*a*) in the case of a liquidated demand, the court otherwise orders, (*b*) in any other case, within seven days after the receipt of the notice of payment into court but not less than two days before the return day, the plaintiff sends to the registrar and every defendant notice that he requires his costs to be taxed. The plaintiff must give notice of his acceptance to the registrar and to the defendants also within seven days of the receipt of the notice of payment into court but not less than two days before the return day (*Ord.* 11, *r.* 7).

Where part payment into court (*a*) is *not* made within fourteen days of service, *or* (*b*) is made within fourteen days *but without costs*, the plaintiff may accept such payment in full satisfaction within seven days after receipt of the notice of payment into court, or, if the notice is received less than seven days before the return day, then before the hearing begins, by giving notice to the defendant and the court. The action is stayed except for the purpose of subsidiary orders and additional costs. The plaintiff is entitled to have the money paid out of court to him if he accepts it within the time limited by the rule (*Ord.* 11, *rr.* 7 (4) and 11), except where *Ord.* 11, *r.* 10 (see below) applies. If the plaintiff accepts the sum paid into court in satisfaction or abandons all other causes of action within the time limited, where *Ord.* 11, *r.* 10, applies, or a party has legal aid, the plaintiff may apply for an order for costs (*Ord.* 11, *r.* 9(*c*)). In any other case, he may lodge a bill for taxation. In the case of the exceptions, he may apply for an order for costs (*Ord.* 11, *r.* 9). The rule is so worded as to apply to a payment into court on account of the claim.

Where the whole amount is paid into court, or part of the amount, **and** *there is a claim for other relief than money*

Payment into court, where there is a claim for other relief than money, should be accompanied by a notice specifying the sum paid in satisfaction of any cause or causes of action in respect of which the defendant desires to make a separate payment (*Ord.* 11, *r.* 3).

Whether the payment is made within or after fourteen days of service, if the plaintiff elects to accept the sum, he must within seven days after receipt by him of the notice of payment into court or, if the notice is received less than seven days before the return day, then before the hearing of the action begins, must give notice of his acceptance to the court and to every defendant. The cause of action in respect of which the payment is made is then stayed. Except in a case to which *Ord.* 11, *r.* 10 (see below) applies, the plaintiff is entitled to have the accepted sum paid out to him without any order of the court, if he accepts it within the time limited by the rule. If, within the time limited for acceptance, the plaintiff also abandons the other causes of action, (*a*) he may apply for an order for the costs incurred by him before the receipt of the notice of payment into court where a party has legal aid or where *Ord.* 11, *r.* 10 (see below) applies, or (*b*) in any other case, he may lodge a bill of costs for taxation, and if the costs allowed are not paid within fourteen days, he may have judgment for them (*Ord.* 11, *r.* 9).

Late acceptance (Ord. 11, r. 11)

If the plaintiff fails to give notice of acceptance within the limited time, he may still give notice at any time before the hearing of the action begins, but an order for payment out of court is required, and the court may order the plaintiff to pay the defendant's costs reasonably incurred since the date of payment into court.

In the case of a claim for money only, where the defendant has also paid into court the appropriate costs on the summons within fourteen days of service, the defendant is not liable for any further costs unless the court otherwise orders.

In the case of a claim for money and another relief, where the plaintiff abandons all outstanding claims, the plaintiff may apply for an order for the costs incurred by him before the receipt of the notice of payment into court. See *Ord. 11, r. 11.*

Sometimes, in simple cases, an order for payment out will be made *ex parte* on an application made by the letter which requests payment out of court, but if the plaintiff wishes to have additional costs, he must obtain an order for them.

Where no payment out, without an order (Ord. 11, r. 10)

An order for payment out of court is also required where payment into court is made:—

(a) by one or more of several defendants sued jointly or in the alternative; or

(b) with a defence of tender before action; or

(c) in an Admiralty action; or

(d) under *Ord. 11, r. 12,* in respect of a claim by a hospital or health insurance society or committee; or

(e) in a proceeding to which *Ord. 5, r. 19* (plaintiff under a disability) or *Ord. 46, r. 12* (Exchange Control Act, 1947), applies.

Costs

If an *order* for costs or additional costs is required to be made, the time for applying for it is when an application is

D

made for payment out of court. Where a party has a certificate
in force entitling him to legal aid, an order for costs may be
required (*Ord.* 11, *rr.* 8 (*e*) and 9 (*c*)).

Where an order for costs is not required, the plaintiff may
lodge his bill of costs for taxation (*Ord.* 11, *rr.* 7 (3A), 8 (*d*)
and 9 (*c*)). If the costs are not paid within fourteen days
after taxation, the plaintiff may have judgment entered for
them and costs of entering judgment. The request for entering
judgment may be by letter. Judgment is in *Form* 68. Costs on
the lower Scale are fixed without taxation (*Ord.* 47, *r.* 37 (1)).

Counterclaim

Where payment is made into court by a defendant who
makes a counterclaim, it must be accompanied by a notice to
show how the counterclaim has been taken into account (*Ord*)
11, *r.* 4). A plaintiff or other person made defendant to a
counterclaim may pay money into court as if he were defendant (*Ord.* 11, *r.* 14).

Forfeiture for non-payment of rent

The procedure for payment into court is modified in the
case of an action for possession on the ground of non-payment
of rent under s. 191 of the Act. If the rent in arrear and costs
are paid into court five clear days before the hearing, the
action ceases.

ADMISSIONS, DEFENCES AND COUNTER-CLAIMS

Order 9 applies to ordinary summonses and *Ord.* 10 to
default summonses.

Legal Aid.—When a party becomes an assisted person under
the Legal Aid (General) Regulations, 1971, his solicitor must
forthwith serve all other parties with notice of the issue of
the certificate for legal aid, and send the certificate by prepaid
post to the court, if the proceedings have begun (*reg.* 17). No
fee on filing.

Ordinary Summons (*Ord.* 9)

Admission.—A defendant who admits the claim or part of it but desires time for payment must within fourteen days of service (inclusive of the day of service) file an admission. The form annexed to the summons may be used. If the admission is received late, it will be accepted before the return day (*Ord.* 9, *r.* 1).

The court may accept as an admission any letter addressed to the court which the court is satisfied was written by or with the authority of the defendant (*Ord.* 9, *r.* 3).

The registrar sends notice of the admission or part-admission to the plaintiff in *Form* 60, together with a copy of the admission or part-admission. If the action is for the delivery of goods under the Hire-Purchase Act, 1965, s. 35, notice in *Form* 61 is sent instead of in *Form* 60.

The notice informs the plaintiff what he must do. He should send notice of acceptance or non-acceptance to the registrar and defendant within eight days, but he may do so at any time until the return day subject to payment of costs properly incurred. If the offer of payment is accepted, and any admission of part of the claim is accepted in satisfaction, the registrar must enter judgment accordingly as soon as practicable. However, in the case of an action for the delivery of goods under the Hire-Purchase Act, 1965, s. 35, where a guarantor is party to the action, judgment will not be entered until the return day (*Ord.* 46, *r.* 10 (3)).

Where the amount admitted is £40 or more, the plaintiff, on sending notice of non-acceptance may require the defendant to give evidence of his means at the hearing. The registrar then sends notice in *Form* 88 to the defendant requiring him to attend to give evidence as to his means, and if he is unable reasonably to attend, then to file an affidavit, which must also state the reasons why he cannot attend. (*Ord.* 9, *r.* 1 (5)).

In an action for recovery of land, if the defendant admits the plaintiff's right to recover possession, the registrar sends notice to the plaintiff in *Form* 62.

Defence and counterclaim.—A defence or counterclaim must be filed within fourteen days of service (inclusive of the day of service). The form annexed to the summons may be used. If this form is not used, the defendant must also lodge with the registrar a copy for every plaintiff. The registrar sends a copy of the defence or counterclaim to the plaintiff. If the defence or counterclaim is filed late, the same procedure is followed.

Fee: on filing counterclaim, the amount by which the plaint fee, which would be payable on the relief counterclaimed, exceeds the plaint fee paid in the action. The fee for service by bailiff is excluded from the calculation.

Any legal aid certificate must be sent to the court and notice of it sent to the other parties forthwith.

Default summons (*Ord.* 10)

Admission.—A defendant, who admits the claim or part of it but desires time for payment, must within fourteen days of service (inclusive of the day of service) file an admission. The form annexed to the summons may be used, but the court may accept any document (which includes a letter) which shows that the defendant desires to ask for time for payment (*Ord.* 10, *r.* 10). If an admission is received late, it will be accepted at any time before judgment (*Ord.* 10, *r.* 2).

If it is not accompanied by a counterclaim, the registrar sends notice of the admission or part-admission to the plaintiff in *Form* 28 (1), together with a copy of the admission or part-admission. The notice informs the plaintiff what he must do. He should send to the court notice of acceptance or non-acceptance within eight days. However, he may do so at any time within twelve months of the date of service of the summons, otherwise, the action is struck out. No extension is allowed (*Ord.* 10, *r.* 7).

If the offer is accepted, and any admission of part of the claim is accepted in satisfaction, the registrar must enter judgment accordingly. Notice of acceptance is usually given by letter, but the *præcipe* for judgment in default, *Form* 30, is convenient. Credit must be given for any sum received on account direct from the defendant to the plaintiff or his solicitor. For costs, see Appendix I, *infra*.

If the offer is not accepted, the registrar sends notice to the plaintiff in *Form* 28 (2), and to the defendant in *Form* 29, of the day fixed for disposal. If the part of the claim admitted is not accepted in satisfaction, the registrar fixes a day for a pre-trial review or, if he thinks fit, a day for hearing, and sends notice to both parties in *Form* 27. In both cases, the length of notice is at least five clear days.

Where the amount admitted is £40 or more, the plaintiff, on sending notice of non-acceptance, may require the defendant to give evidence of his means at the disposal, hearing or a pre-trial review. The registrar sends notice in *Form* 88 to the defendant requiring him to give evidence as to his means as in the case of an ordinary summons (see above) (*Ord*. 10, *r*. 4 (4)).

If a notice of admission contains *no offer* of the manner of payment, it is usual to set the matter down for disposal. Practice varies when a notice of admission is *not signed*. The better practice appears to be to set the action down for disposal and to leave it to the plaintiff to take what steps he thinks are best suited to the circumstances of the case, for "admission" means any document which shows that the defendant desires to ask for time for payment (*Ord*. 10, *r*. 10).

Defence and counterclaim.—A defence or counterclaim must be filed within fourteen days of service (inclusive of the day of service). The form annexed to the summons may be used. If this form is not used, the defendant must also lodge with the registrar a copy for every plaintiff. A defence or counterclaim will be accepted at any time before judgment is entered. The registrar fixes a day for a pre-trial review or, if he thinks fit, a day for hearing, and gives not less than eight clear days' notice of it in *Form* 27, sending a copy of the defence and counterclaim to the plaintiff (*Ord*. 10, *rr*. 1 and 3).

Fee: on filing counterclaim, the amount by which the plaint fee, which would be payable on the relief counterclaimed, exceeds the plaint fee paid in the action. The fee for service by bailiff is excluded from the calculation.

Any legal aid certificate must be sent to the court and notice of it sent to the other parties forthwith.

Judgment in default.—If an admission, defence or counter-claim is not filed within the fourteen days, and the defendant does not pay the debt and costs, the plaintiff may enter judgment (*Ord.* 10, *r.* 2), but he must do so within twelve months of the day of service (*Ord.* 10, *r.* 7).

Requirements:

    (*a*) *Præcipe* in *Form* 30 (supplied by the court);

    (*b*) Plaint note;

    (*c*) Stamped addressed envelope, if by post.

No fee. Additional costs: judgment over £5 to £20, 50p; over £20 to £100, £1; over £100, £1.50 but if amount claimed is £75 or less, only costs on summons are allowed. There is an item in the Rules for costs on judgment for amounts under £75.

The order for payment may be made forthwith, in which case no order is sent to the defendant and execution may issue at the same time. If payment is to be made in one sum on a certain day (e.g., in seven days), or by instalments, the registrar sends to the defendant judgment in *Form* 131 or 132, as the case may be.

General

Defective admissions and defences.—If an admission or defence is signed in a different name from that of a defendant, some county courts will amend the name on an application by letter (*fee* (No. 8), 50p). However, some such amendments are better left until the hearing (in which case there is no fee), or dealt with by a formal application on notice. Some cases will involve the substitution of a defendant. In some cases, the signature may be that of a wife of a defendant, and this is sometimes accepted as a wife acting as agent for her husband. Some courts return admissions and defences which are signed in a name which is not consistent with the name of the defendant, or which are not signed at all. There is no rule on the subject and practice varies.

INTERLOCUTORY APPLICATIONS
General

The basic procedure is set out in *Ord.* 13, *r.* 1.

Requirements, if application to be made on notice:

(a) *Form* Ex. 23 and copy;

(b) *Fee*, if payable, usually 50p if made before hearing or judgment (*Fee* No. 8);

(c) Affidavit, if any;

(d) Plaint note or originating process, to be marked with any fee paid;

(e) Stamped addressed envelope if by post.

For *Form* Ex. 23, see Appendix IV, *infra*, and *County Court Practice*, after County Court Forms, editorial Form (D).

The place, date and time of hearing are completed and one copy is returned for service. If a defendant in person is making the application the court often serves the copy.

An application may be made either in, or out of, court, and either *ex parte*, or on notice.

Where made on notice: (a) the notice must be in writing and must be served on the opposite party and filed in the court not less than one clear day before the hearing unless the judge or registrar dispenses with notice or gives leave for short notice; and (b) the party serving the notice must be responsible for ascertaining that the judge or registrar will be available to hear the application.

No affidavit is necessary in the first instance, unless an Act or rule so requires.

If the registrar has power to hear and determine the application, the applicant must, unless the judge otherwise orders, make the application to the registrar in the first instance.

Where the application is made to the registrar, he may, if in doubt as to the proper order to be made, refer the application to the judge forthwith or at the next convenient opportunity, and the judge may hear the application and make such order as may be just.

The costs of an interlocutory application are not taxed until the general taxation of the costs of the action or matter, unless the judge or registrar otherwise orders, and where an earlier taxation is ordered, *Ord.* 47 (which applies to costs) applies as if the word "claimed" were substituted for the word "recovered" (*Ord.* 13, r. 1 (1)).

The form of application, known as Ex. 23, may be used for *ex parte* applications, and then the date is left blank. An application by letter is now generally accepted when no appointment is required. Some *ex parte* applications are required to be made by affidavit, in which case the affidavit alone is sufficient, as in the case of substituted service. In other cases, the application is made at the time of taking some proceedings, and then the order or leave is marked on the *præcipe* or form required, as in the case of leave to issue execution "after two years". Practice varies.

"Court" implies judge *or* registrar (*Ord.* 48, *r.* 4).

Directions

The court may at any time on the application on notice of any party or of its own motion give directions (*Ord.* 13, *r.* 3 (1)). For pre-trial review, see *infra*.

An order for directions is in *Form* 368 (*Ord*, 13, *r.* 3).

Adjournment

The court may upon application or of its own motion adjourn or advance the date of hearing of any proceeding. Notice of such adjournment or advancement (*Form* 71) is given by the registrar to all parties who are not present when the order is made (*Ord.* 13, *r.* 4), although it is now common practice to send notice to those parties who were present. No fee on application to adjourn, but a *fee* of 50p is payable on an application to advance the hearing.

Many applications for adjournments are made *ex parte* on filing written consent of all parties. A reason for the adjournment is usually expected to be given. If the application is late, the party may have to apply in open court, or to the judge if he was to hear the action. In debt collecting actions, and according to circumstances, an adjournment is sometimes granted on the request of the plaintiff by letter without a signed consent from the defendant. Practice varies. An application to adjourn may always be made on notice.

An application to restore an action to the list for hearing after being adjourned *sine die* is usually made by letter. No fee. Notice of the new hearing (*Form* 72) is sent by the court.

If an action is not restored within twelve months, it may be struck out following a notice in *Form* 67 being sent by the court.

Further particulars of claim

Order. 7, *r.* 9, applies.

If a defendant requires further particulars of the claim, he must file a notice specifying what further particulars he requires and deliver a copy of the notice to the plaintiff. The rule requires this to be done within eight days of the service of the summons. It also requires the plaintiff to file the further particulars of his claim and deliver a copy to the defendant within five days of service of the notice. No forms of notice are prescribed, but see editorial Form (E) in *County Court Practice*, after the County Court Forms.

If the plaintiff does not comply with the notice, the defendant may apply to the registrar for an order.

Requirements:

(*a*) Notice of application in *Form* Ex. 23 and copy for service.

(*b*) *Fee:* 50p.

Form of application, see editorial Form (F) in *County Court Practice*, after the County Court Forms.

Application may also be made in the procedure for pre-trial review under *Ord.* 21.

If the order provides that the action be dismissed on the plaintiff not complying with it, it is advisable, in the event of non-compliance, to apply again for a definite order that the action be dismissed.

Further particulars of defence

Order. 9, *r.* 4(6), and *Ord.* 10, *r.* 9, apply.

If the plaintiff requires further particulars of the defence, he must file a notice specifying what further particulars he requires and deliver a copy to the defendant. The defendant must then file the further particulars and deliver a copy to the plaintiff within five days. No forms of notice are prescribed, but see editorial Forms (E) and (F) in *County Court*

Practice, after the County Court Forms. If the defendant does not comply with the notice, the plaintiff may apply to the registrar for an order accordingly.

Requirements:

  (*a*) Notice of application in *Form* Ex. 23 and copy for service;

  (*b*) *Fee:* 50p.

Application may also be made in the procedure for pre-trial review under *Ord.* 21.

If the order provides that the defendant be debarred from defending, it is advisable, in the event of non-compliance, to apply again for a definite order.

Interlocutory judgment where defendant debarred

Where a defendant is debarred from defending altogether or the whole of his defence is struck out, the plaintiff may have judgment entered for his claim and costs (*Ord.* 24, *r.* 10 (1). If the claim is for unliquidated damages, the judgment is an interlocutory judgment (*Form* 127 (1)) for damages to be assessed and costs. An application for assessment of damages is made on notice under the procedure for interlocutory applications under *Ord.* 13, *r.* 1. Final judgment is in *Form* 127 (2) (*Ord.* 24, *r.* 10 (2) and (3)).

Discovery

Order. 14, *r.* 2, applies.

Any party may give notice in writing to any other party requiring him to make discovery on oath of the documents relating to any question in the proceedings, which may be or have been in his possession or power. No form of notice is prescribed.

If the party does not comply with the notice within three days, application may be made to the registrar for an order.

Requirements:

  (*a*) Notice of application in *Form* Ex. 23 and copy for service;

  (*b*) *Fee:* 50p.

The court may make an order notwithstanding that prior

notice has not been given, where it is satisfied that there were reasonable grounds for not giving it.

Form of order is in *Form* 82 (drawn by the court). Affidavit or list of documents is in *Form* 83 (not supplied by the court). Order is served by the applicant.

Application may also be made in the procedure for pre-trial review under *Ord.* 21.

Inspection of documents

Order. 14, *r.* 3, applies.

Application may be made in the procedure for pre-trial review under *Ord.* 21. *Forms* 84, 85 and 86 are applicable. *Forms* 84 and 85 are not supplied by the court.

Interrogatories

Order. 14, *r.* 1, applies.

Any party may apply to the registrar on notice for leave to deliver interrogatories in writing.

Requirements:

(*a*) Notice of application in *Form* Ex. 23 and copy for service;

(*b*) Proposed interrogatories and copy for service;

(*c*) *Fee:* 50p.

Order is in *Form* 80 and is served by the applicant.

Interrogatories must be answered by affidavit.

No reasonable cause of action

The court may order the whole or part of any particulars of claim or defence to be amended or struck out on the ground that it discloses no reasonable cause of action or defence, or it is scandalous, frivolous or vexatious, or it may prejudice, embarrass or delay the fair trial, or it is otherwise an abuse of the process of the court. The court may order the action to be stayed or dismissed or judgment to be entered accordingly. An application for an order must be made on notice. (*Ord.* 13, *r.* 6).

Order for detention or preservation of property, etc.

Order. 13, *r.* 11, applies.

Application may be made to the registrar for an order for

the detention, preservation, inspection, surveying, measuring, or weighing of any property being the subject matter of the action. Rules as to interlocutory applications apply, but a draft form of order must be prepared beforehand and settled by the registrar except where the case is one of urgency (*Ord.* 13, *r.* 13).

The court has power to protect goods under the Hire-Purchase Act, 1965, *s.* 35 (3).

Inspection and preservation of property which may become the subject of subsequent proceedings.
Discovery and inspection before commencement of proceedings and after commencement in respect of persons who are not parties.

The Administration of Justice Act, 1969, s. 21, provides for inspection, preservation, etc., of property which may become the subject-matter of subsequent proceedings.

The Administration of Justice Act, 1970, ss. 31 and 32, refer to actions for personal injuries and in respect of a person's death. Section 31 provides for the disclosure and inspection of documents in the possession of a person likely to be a party, before the commencement of the proceedings. Section 32 (1) provides for disclosure and inspection of documents in the possession of a person who is not a party, after the commencement of an action. Section 32 (2) provides for the inspection, preservation, etc., of property not in the possession of a party, after the commencement of an action, and seems to apply only to actions for personal injuries and not to other types of action as notes in the *Supreme Court Practice* seem to imply.

R.S.C., *Ord.* 24, *r.* 7A, and *Ord.* 29, *r.* 7A, are applied with necessary modifications by C.C.R., *Ord.* 13, *r.* 15.

As to the production and inspection of documents in the possession of a non-party in an action other than for personal injuries after the commencement of an action, *Ord.* 20, *r.* 18, applies (*cf.* R.S.C., *Ord.* 38, *r.* 13).

Interim payment of damages

The Administration of Justice Act, 1969, s. 20, gives power

for county court rules to be made for enabling the court to make an order for the interim payment of damages before final judgment or order.

No county court rules have yet been made, but rules have been made in the High Court. These rules are R.S.C., *Ord.* 29, *rr.* 9 to 17.

Interim injunction

Order 13, *r.* 8, applies.

Application for an injunction is to a judge, except where the Hire-Purchase Act, 1965, s. 35(3), applies under *Ord.* 46, *r.* 10(2), and then the application may be made to a registrar.

An application may be made before or after the trial or hearing (*Ord.* 13, *r.* 8(1) and (2)) and should be made on notice. An application for an injunction may be made *ex parte* in the case of urgency (*ibid.*). As to degree of urgency, note *Bates* v· *Lord Hailsham* [1972] 3 All E.R. 1019. The applicant or his solicitor or counsel is expected to attend before the judge. In the case of urgency, the application may be made before the issue of the proceedings (*Ord.* 13, *r.* 8(3)).

Application filed *at the same time as the issue* of the proceedings—requirements:

(a) Request or *præcipe* (or originating application or petition and copy for service);

(b) Particulars of claim (in the case of an action) and copy for each defendant;

(c) If plaintiff under disability, undertaking by next friend (*Form* 12) (if applicable);

(d) Legal aid certificate, if any, and notice of certificate (for service);

(e) Application for injunction in *Form* Ex. 23 and copy for service (may be dispensed with if application is being made *ex parte*);

(f) Affidavit in support (plaintiff will require a copy for service on defendant when application made on notice);

(g) Draft order in *Form* 79 (which is to be settled by registrar) except in the case of urgency;

(*h*) *Fees:* plaint fee and fee for service by bailiff, if bailiff serves; for application, 50p.

A plaint note is issued by the court.

After issue of proceedings, requirements:
(*a*) Application in *Form* Ex. 23 and copy for service;
(*b*) Affidavit in support (plaintiff requires a copy for service);
(*c*) Draft order in *Form* 79 (which is to be settled by registrar) except in case of urgency;
(*d*) *Fee:* 50p.

Before issue of proceedings—exceptional—requirements:
(*a*) Affidavit in support also showing that court has jurisdiction to hear and determine the proposed action;
(*b*) Proposed particulars of claim (or originating application or petition, as the case may be);
(*c*) *Fee:* 50p.

In this case, if an injunction is granted, it must be on terms for the issue of the action or matter (*Ord.* 13, *r.* 8(3)).

When an application is made on notice, the rule does not specifically state that an affidavit is necessary, but an affidavit is usually filed following the practice in the High Court. The notice of application must be served on the opposite parties at least one clear day before the hearing (*Ord.* 13, *r.* 1(*b*)), but two clear days in the case of matrimonial proceedings (M.C.R. *r.* 114).

If the notice of application for an interim injunction is filed at the same time as the issue of the summons, arrangements should be made for the summons to be served before or with the notice of application.

Except where the case is one of urgency, the draft of the order should be prepared beforehand and settled by the registrar, and if the judge grants the application, he may sign the order so settled or with such alterations as he thinks proper (*Ord.* 13, *r.* 13). The signed order is delivered to the registrar who issues sealed copies for service. *Fee:* for service by bailiff, 50p.

Other Interim Orders

Order 13 provides for other interlocutory orders, such as enlargement or abridgement of time (*r.* 5), security for costs where defendant does not reside within twenty miles from the court (*r.* 7), recovery of goods where lien claimed (*r.* 9), preservation, inspection, etc., of property (*rr.* 10 and 11), for sale of perishables (*r.* 12).

PRELIMINARY CONSIDERATION OF ACTION OR MATTER; PRE-TRIAL REVIEW (*Ord.* 21)

The procedure for a pre-trial review is contained in *Ord.* 21 and applies where a return day is fixed for this purpose on the issue of an ordinary summons, or on the filing of a defence, counterclaim or part-admission in a default action.

In any proceeding in which no pre-trial review has been fixed, the registrar may nevertheless give notice to the parties in *Form* 367 requiring them to appear before him on the day named in the notice so that the question of giving directions might be considered (*Ord.* 21, *r.* 10). Such notice might be given in an originating application under the Married Women's Property Act, 1882, s. 17.

On a pre-trial review, the registrar must consider the course of the proceedings and give all necessary or desirable directions. He must endeavour to secure that the parties make such admissions and agreements as are reasonable. Every party must, so far as practicable, apply for any particular direction he may desire on giving notice to the registrar and other parties. Rules as to interlocutory applications apply.

Affidavit evidence may be given on the pre-trial review (*Ord.* 21, *r.* 5).

If the defendant admits the claim or such part thereof as the plaintiff accepts in satisfaction, the registrar may proceed as on a disposal and enter judgment. (*Ord.* 21, *r.* 6).

If the defendant does not appear and has not delivered an admission or defence, the registrar may enter judgment for the plaintiff (*Ord.* 21, *r.* 7). The rule does not say whether evidence is to be given, but evidence by affidavit may be given in an ordinary action without an order, where no defence is filed pursuant to *Ord.* 20, *r.* 5(2).

If the defendant does not appear but has delivered a defence, the registrar may, if the plaintiff so requests, exercise his powers under *Ord.* 23, *r.* 4, that is, he may give judgment on proof of service and of the facts (*Ord.* 21, *r.* 8). If the defendant does not appear, the registrar may, nevertheless, give directions.

Interlocutory judgment for damages may also be entered on a pre-trial review (*Ord.* 24, *r.* 10 (4)). However, if judgment is given at the pre-trial review, judgment may also be given for the amount of damages if the plaintiff adduces evidence (*Ord.* 24, *r.* 10 (4)).

If the plaintiff does not appear on a return day which has been fixed for a pre-trial review, the proceedings must be struck out, unless the court has received an affidavit from him (*Ord.* 23, *r.* 2).

If the pre-trial review proceeds, on or as soon as practicable after completing his consideration, the registrar must, if the action remains to be tried, fix a day for the trial and give notice to all parties (*Ord.* 21, *r.* 9). *Order* 21 does not provide for a form of order or prescribe a form of notice of trial. An order for directions would be in *Form* 368. An application to refer the proceedings to arbitration under *Ord.* 19, *r.* 1, may also be dealt with.

THIRD PARTY PROCEDURE (*Ord.* 12)

Application for leave to issue a third party notice must be made by application on notice.

Requirements:

(*a*) Notice of application in *Form* Ex 23 and copy for service;

(*b*) Copy of third party notice (*Form* 70, not supplied);

(*c*) *Fee:* 50p (No. 8);

(*d*) Stamped addressed envelope, if by post.

All other proceedings in the action are stayed until the hearing of the application (*Ord.* 12, *r.* 1(2)). The court returns one copy of the notice of application, completed with the date of hearing. It is not sealed. The copy (with a copy of the third party notice) should be served on the plaintiff within eight days of service of the summons, and at least one clear day before the hearing of the application, and all other proceedings in the action are stayed. Applications for third party notice are usually filed and served after the eight days. Application to extend time may be made in the application or earlier and *ex parte* if necessary. Notice of the application is not served on the proposed third party.

If leave is granted, the court gives directions as to time for service and further conduct of the proceedings. Judgment in default may not be entered in a default action pending trial.

Two copies of the third party notice are prepared, one for service and one for endorsement or for an exhibit to the affidavit of service. Apparently it is not necessary to seal the notices, although in practice they usually are sealed. A copy of the summons and particulars of claim must be annexed to the copy for service, and also any notice of adjournment or other notice of hearing. *Fee:* for service by bailiff, 50p.

A third party may similarly apply for leave to issue a fourth party notice, and so on (*Ord.* 12, *r.* 4).

Where a defendant makes against any other defendant in the same action such a claim that could be made the subject of third party proceedings, he may without leave issue and serve on such other defendant a notice making such a claim (*Ord.* 12, *r.* 5). A copy of the notice should be filed with the court.

After judgment, execution may not be issued against a third party without leave of the judge until the defendant has satisfied the judgment against him (*Ord.* 12, *r.* 3(2) proviso). A registrar may give leave if judgment was given by him (*Ord.* 48, *r.* 5), but this may be questioned.

AMENDMENT

Order 15 deals with amendment and *Ord.* 15, *r.* 1, is the general rule.

General.—The court may at any time (*a*) amend any defects

E

and errors in any proceedings whether the defect or error is that of the party applying to amend or not; and (*b*) add, strike out or substitute any person either as plaintiff or defendant; and all such amendments as may be necessary for the purpose of determining the real question in controversy, provided that no person may be added as plaintiff without his consent in writing, or in the case of a person under disability without the consent in writing of the next friend or other person acting on his behalf (*Ord.* **15,** *r.* **1).**

The "slip rule" is *Ord.* **15,** *r.* **12.**

Requirements, *where no other procedure prescribed:*

    (*a*) Application in *Form* Ex. 23 and copy for service;

    (*b*) *Fee:* 50p if made before judgment or hearing.

Amendment before service. Where there is an error in the *præcipe, Ord.* 8, *r.* 29, applies; see *supra.*

Amendment of particulars of claim and of defence.—Amended particulars of claim or an amended defence or counterclaim may be filed at any time before the hearing on payment of any balance of plaint fee due on any increased claim. A copy of the amended pleading is sent direct by the party filing to the other parties. The copy does not have to be sealed (*Ord.* 15, *r.* 4).

In a default action where the plaintiff's claim is amended by adding or substituting a claim which could not have been made in a default action, the action continues as if it had been commenced as an ordinary action (*Ord.* 15, *r.* 5).

Change in parties **before** *judgment.*—Order 5, *rr.* 36 to 39, apply, where there is any assignment, creation, change, transmission or devolution of the interest, estate, or title, or liability.

Requirements:

    (*a*) Notice in *Form* 108, or, if more than one action or matter, *Form* 110 may be used, with as many copies of notice as there are parties to be served;

    (*b*) Affidavit of truth of facts;

    (*c*) *Fee:* 25p, but no fee if change is "by operation of law", and presumably in addition 5p for every action more than one (No. 37).

The court sends notice in *Form* 109 and a copy of the notice in *Form* 108.

In the case of a change in the plaintiff's title, the person upon whom the title has devolved applies. In the case of a change in the defendant's title, the person, upon whom the title has devolved, or the plaintiff, may give notice. Where notice is to be served on a person to be substituted or added as a defendant, a copy of the originating process must be annexed to the notice (*Ord.* 5, *r.* 37).

Where a plaintiff or defendant dies and the cause of action survives, but the person entitled to proceed fails to proceed, the defendant (or the person against whom the proceedings may be continued) may apply for an order directing the plaintiff (or other person entitled) to proceed within such time as may be ordered, and in default, the action may be struck out (*Ord.* 5, *r.* 38).

The bankruptcy of the plaintiff in an action which the trustee might maintain for the benefit of the creditors does not cause the action to abate if, within such reasonable time as the court orders, the trustee elects to continue the action and to give security. When the trustee does not elect to continue the action and to give security, the defendant may use the bankruptcy as a defence (County Courts Act, 1959, s. 82).

Change in parties **after** *judgment.—Order* 25, *r.* 6, applies, where any change has taken place after judgment by death, assignment or otherwise, in the parties entitled to enforce a judgment or order or in the parties liable under a judgment or order.

Requirements:
   (*a*) If *ex parte*, affidavit, applying for leave to issue enforcement process;
   (*b*) *Fee:* 25p; if more than one judgment, then 5p in addition for every additional judgment (No. 37).

No fee, where change is "by operation of law".

If the application affects more than one judgment, one application may be made specifying judgments in a schedule.

Order is in *Form* 151, or, if more than one judgment, in *Form* 152. Order is drawn by the court.

If order made *ex parte*, no process may issue until the expiration of seven days after service of the order.

Order 5, *r.* 40, applies where there is money in court.

In an action for recovery of land, any person not named as a defendant may by leave be allowed to appear on filing an affidavit with copies for all parties not less than five clear days before the return day, showing that he is in possession by himself or by his tenant. If leave is given, the applicant is added as a defendant and the court sends notice in *Form* 89 to all parties, annexing to it a copy of the affidavit (*Ord.* 15, *r.* 10). In the case of summary proceedings for recovery of land, *Ord.* 26, *r.* 4, also applies (see *ante*).

TRANSFER OF PROCEEDINGS

Transfer to another county court

If the registrar or judge is satisfied that any proceedings can be more conveniently or fairly tried in some other court, he may order them to be transferred to that court (*Ord.* 16, *r.* 1 (1)).

Where a defendant does not reside or carry on business within the district of the court and he desires the action to be transferred to the court for the district in which he resides or carries on business, he may apply *ex parte* in writing *without fee* for an order to transfer the action to that court. If the judge or registrar, after considering the question whether the claim is disputed, thinks that it would be a *hardship* on the defendant for the action to proceed in the court in which it was commenced, he may order the action to be transferred. Before dealing with the application, the judge or registrar may cause notice to be given to the plaintiff that the application has been made and of a day and hour when the plaintiff may attend and be heard, and, if necessary, may adjourn the hearing of the action. The application is usually made in the defence, and some courts, instead of giving the plaintiff an appointment in the first place, will write to him or his solicitor to ask if he consents to the transfer (*Ord.* 16, *r.* 1 (2)).

Proceedings may be transferred, when the judge has an interest in the subject matter (*Ord.* 16, *r.* 2), when any party is an officer of the court (*Ord.* 16, *r.* 3), and when the registrar, his partner or clerk has acted in proceedings transferred from the High Court (*Ord.* 16, *r.* 5).

Where proceedings are commenced in the wrong court, such as when the address of the defendant is found to be out of the district of the court, the judge or registrar may either—

(*a*) transfer the proceedings to the court in which they ought to have been commenced; or

(*b*) order that they shall continue in the court in which they were commenced; or

(*c*) order them to be struck out (*Ord.* 16, *r.* 4).

Where a summons has been issued in the wrong court because an address, which was thought to be within its district, is found to be outside it, the practice of some courts is to request the plaintiff to withdraw the proceedings and then to re-commence them in the correct court. The plaint fee is then returned on production of the plaint note of the new action, but regard should be had to the Statutes of Limitation.

An order to transfer may be made by the court on its own motion, or on the application of any party on not less than three clear days' notice (*Ord.* 16, *r.* 6). Form of application *Form* Ex. 23; *fee* 50p.

Order of transfer is in *Form* 90. A certified copy of the entries in the court books is sent with the papers to the court to which the proceedings are transferred; *fee* payable thereon: 5p, being paid by the plaintiff when the court transfers on its own motion. The court to which the action is transferred sends notice of hearing or pre-trial review in *Form* 91 (*Ord.* 16 *rr.* 6 to 8).

The judge may at any time, upon application or upon his own motion, direct that the hearing of proceedings pending in his own court, being proceedings which are to be heard and determined by him, shall take place in some other court of which he is the judge. Notice of hearing is given by the court in *Form* 87 (*Ord.* 13, *r.* 4A). This is not a transfer of proceedings. The procedure is sometimes followed when a "branch" county court has a long defended action which is more conveniently heard at the judge's main court in some large town.

Funds.—The court may, at any time, on application in that behalf or on its own motion, order any money invested as funds in court under *Ord.* 5, *r.* 19 (2), or s. 174 of the Act ("infants' settlements") to be transferred to another county court. Application can be made by letter; no fee.

Judgment summons and attachment of earnings.—An order for transfer may be made under *Ord.* 25, *r.* 48, and *Ord.* 25 *r.* 79 (4); see, *infra.*

Transfer to the High Court

Proceedings may be transferred to the High Court in the following instances:

County Courts Act, 1959

In an action founded on *contract or tort* where the plaintiff claims damages, the plaintiff may apply to the judge for an order to transfer the action to the High Court on the ground that there are reasonable grounds for supposing the amount recoverable will be in excess of the county court jurisdiction (s. 43).

In an action founded on *contract or tort* where the plaintiff claims a sum exceeding £100, the defendant may give notice that he objects to the action being tried in the county court. The judge must order the action to be transferred to the High Court if the defendant gives security and the judge certifies that some important question of law or fact is likely to arise (s. 44). Notice of objection must be delivered to the court and the plaintiff within fourteen days of service of the summons (inclusive of the day of service). The application must be made to the judge accompanied by an affidavit in *Form* 100. Notice to the plaintiff of the judge's certificate is given in *Form* 101 (*Ord.* 16, *r.* 18).

In an action for the *recovery of land*, the defendant or his landlord may apply to a judge of the High Court in chambers for the plaintiff to show cause why the action should not be transferred to the High Court on the ground that the title to

land having a net annual value for rating exceeding £1000 would
be affected by the decision in the action (s. 49). Application
must be made within fourteen days of service of the summons
(inclusive of the day of service) (*Ord.* 16, *r.* 17). Application
may be made to a master, or to a district registrar if the county
court is within the district of his district registry (R.S.C.,
Ord. 107, *r.* 1).

In *Admiralty proceedings*, any party may apply to the
High Court for an order of transfer (s. 58 (1)). If, during the
progress of any Admiralty proceedings, it appears to the
county court that the proceedings could be more conveniently
prosecuted in the High Court, the county court may make an
order for transfer (s. 58 (2)).

In *counterclaims*, which involve matters beyond the jurisdiction of a county court, any party may apply to the High
Court for an order of transfer (s. 65). The application must be
made, by a plaintiff within eight days after receipt of the
counterclaim, or, by a defendant within eight days of the
delivery of it (R.S.C., *Ord.* 107, *r.* 2).

In proceedings where the county court has *no jurisdiction*,
the county court must transfer the proceedings to the High
Court unless jurisdiction is given by consent under ss. 42, 53
and 56(5), but a defendant may apply to have the action
struck out on the grounds that the plaintiff knew or ought to
have known that the court did not have jurisdiction (s. 66).

The High Court may transfer an action to itself when
an application is made for the *examination of witnesses
abroad* (s. 85). The power to transfer may be exercised by "a
master of the Queen's Bench Division" (R.S.C., *Ord.* 107, *r.* 3).

Crown Proceedings Act, 1947, *s.* 20

In proceedings against the Crown, if there is produced a
certificate of the Attorney-General to the effect that the
proceedings may involve an important question of law, or
may be decisive of other cases arising out of the same matter,
or are for other reasons more fit to be tried in the High Court,
the proceedings may be removed to the High Court. Application is made to the High Court.

Other enactments

Guardianship of Minors Act, 1971, s. 16 (1).—Any party may apply to the High Court for an order to remove any application under the Act to the High Court. R.S.C., *Ord.* 90, *r.* 10, applies.

Landlord and Tenant Act, 1954, s. 63.—Any party may apply for an order to transfer the proceedings to the High Court. If all parties agree to transfer, no order is required (*Ord.* 40, *r.* 12). *Order* 40, *r.* 12, and R.S.C., *Ord.* 97, *r.* 11, apply. It appears that the transfer must be to the High Court in London.

Married Women's Property Act, 1882, s. 17.—Proceedings under this Act may be transferred to the High Court under M.C.R., *r.* 104A. They also may be removed by certiorari under this section or under the County Courts Act, 1959, s. 115. *Order* 16, *r.* 20, applies.

Matrimonial Causes Act, 1973, s. 45.—Legitimacy proceedings: if the county court considers that the case is one which owing to the value of property involved or otherwise ought to be dealt with by the High Court, it may, or if so ordered by the High Court, it must transfer the proceedings. *Order* 39, *r.* 11 (2), applies. The transfer must be to London. This section replaces s. 39 (3) of the Matrimonial Causes Act, 1965.

Equity proceedings

In equity proceedings, where it appears that the subject-matter exceeds the jurisdiction, or the registrar, on taking an account or making an inquiry, certifies that the subject-matter exceeds the jurisdiction, and the judge is of opinion that the excess exists, the judge must transfer the proceedings to the High Court unless there is an agreement to the jurisdiction under s. 66 of the Act. Before presenting the certificate, the registrar may complete the inquiry (*Ord.* 16, *r.* 16).

Procedure

In an application to the High Court, a district registrar has power to transfer proceedings in a county court to the High Court if the district for which the county court is held is comprised in the district of his registry (R.S.C., *Ord.* 107, *r.* 1(3)). The application is made by originating summons. A district registrar may not make an order of certiorari.

The procedure in the county court is set out in *Ord.* 16, *r.* 19.

If there is money in court, the registrar should send a letter to the Chief Accountant, Supreme Court Pay Office, Royal Courts of Justice, London WC2A 2LL informing him that the money is in the county court and should be transferred.

Certiorari and prohibition, see, *infra*.

Transfer from the High Court

Transfer of actions and matters from the High Court to a county court is provided for in the County Courts Act, 1959.

Section 45 applies to actions founded on *contract* or *tort*, and these actions, commenced in the High Court, may on the application of either party at any time be transferred to a county court where the amount in dispute or remaining in dispute does not exceed £750. This applies whether the action could, or could not, have been commenced in the county court, and also, whether there is a counterclaim or an intended counterclaim, either in contract or tort, exceeding or not exceeding £750. If there only remains a counterclaim to be tried and the amount claimed thereby or remaining in dispute does not exceed £750, such counterclaim may be transferred.

The order may be for transfer to any county court in which the action or counterclaim (if it had been an action) might have been commenced if the subject-matter and amount thereof had been within the jurisdiction of the court, or to any county court which the High Court may deem the most convenient.

With regard to other actions within the jurisdiction of county courts, s. 50 provides for the transfer of actions for *recovery of land*, s. 54 for the transfer of proceedings in the *Chancery* Division and s. 59 for the transfer of *Admiralty* proceedings.

Section 68 provides for the transfer of *interpleader* proceedings to a county court. The limit of jurisdiction is £750.

Section 146 applies to the transfer of proceedings for the attachment of a debt (*garnishee*) or an issue as to the liability of an alleged partner in a firm. The limit of jurisdiction is £750.

Section 67 applies to the transfer of proceedings to a county court in excess of its jurisdiction by agreement. A Queen's Bench action, for any amount, will be transferred to a county court if the parties agree by a memorandum in writing signed by them or their solicitors, to any county court specified in the memorandum (see s. 42). Similar provisions apply to Chancery actions (see s. 53) and to Admiralty actions (see s. 56 (5)), and under the Landlord and Tenant Act, 1954, s. 63 (3).

Where leave is given to enter judgment for part of the claim, and the residue is transferred to the county court, judgment for the part is entered in the High Court.

Setting down in county court.—The party having conduct of the proceedings, usually the plaintiff, requests the High Court (often, a district registry) to send all documents filed or lodged in the action to the county court.

Requirements in county court:—

    (*a*) Statement of parties—names and addresses of parties and solicitors; ordinary summons *præcipe* can be used;

    (*b*) Writ, or copy of it, if no copy is received from the High Court;

    (*c*) Order of transfer, or copy;

    (*d*) Any agreement that the county court shall have jurisdiction;

    (*e*) Particulars of claim, and a copy for each other party, unless the statement of claim is fully endorsed on the writ; copies for other parties are not required if they have already been served with statement of claim;

(*f*) If the party lodging is defendant and only counter-claim is transferred and the counterclaim has not been served and delivered, particulars of the counterclaim with copy for each plaintiff;

(*g*) Any legal aid documents;

(*h*) Where money has been paid into High Court, copy of the notice of payment into court;

(*j*) Copy of any other pleading served and delivered whilst the action was proceeding in the High Court, for instance, any defence;

(*k*) Stamped addressed envelope, if by post;

(*l*) *Fee, £2* (No. 17).

(Section 77 of the Act and *Ord.* 16, *r.* 10).

A plaint note and notice of hearing in *Form* 92 are given to a plaintiff setting down. Notice of hearing in *Form* 93 is sent to the other parties by the court by post. The court gives not less than twenty-one clear days' notice of the hearing. A copy of the particulars of claim, if any filed, is annexed to the notice sent to the defendant.

Where the party setting down does not reside or carry on business within England and Wales, he must give security for costs or an undertaking by a solicitor must be filed, as on the issue of an ordinary summons unless the court otherwise orders.

Where no defence has been served or delivered in the High Court, the defendant must within fourteen days of the receipt of the notice of hearing deliver at the court office a statement of his defence, and, if the defendant has a counter-claim, particulars thereof, together with a copy for every plaintiff (*Ord.* 16, *r.* 10).

Where the *trial of an issue* is to be heard, *Ord.* 16, *r.* 10 (8), applies.

Service on an added or substituted defendant has to be personal and *Ord.* 16, *r.* 10 (9), applies.

In *interpleader proceedings, Ord.* 16, *r.* 11, applies.

Transfer of funds from the High Court *for investment, Ord.* 16, *rr.* 13 to 15, and *County Court Funds Rules,* 1965, *r.* 12 *et seq.,* apply.

CONSOLIDATION OF PROCEEDINGS AND SELECTED ACTIONS

Actions or matters pending in the same court may be consolidated by order of the judge or registrar of his own motion or on the application of any party on notice (*Ord.* 17, *r.* 1). Application may be in *Form* Ex. 23. *Fee:* 50p. Form of order is *Form* 54.

If one action is pending in another court, application can be made for its transfer for the purpose of the order.

As to the selection of an action from several actions for trial, arising out of the same circumstances, *Ord.* 17, *rr.* 2 to 5, apply. *Forms* 55 to 57 apply.

DISCONTINUANCE (*Ord.* 18)

The term "withdrawal" is customarily used for discontinuance.

If a plaintiff desires to discontinue wholly or in part any proceedings against all or any of the parties thereto, he should give notice in *Form* 58 to the court and to every party against whom he desires to discontinue (*Ord.* 18, *r.* 1). The form is not supplied by the court. Most usually discontinuance is notified by letter. If a hearing is pending, the court should be notified without delay—a special sitting may have been arranged.

After receiving notice of discontinuance, a party may, unless the judge on the application of a plaintiff otherwise orders, lodge for taxation a bill of costs incurred by him before the receipt of the notice, or, if the proceedings are not wholly discontinued, his costs incurred before the receipt of the notice in relation to the part discontinued. If the costs allowed on taxation are not paid within fourteen days after taxation, the party may have judgment entered for them and the costs of entering judgment. Judgment is in *Form* 59 and is drawn by the court. If the proceedings are not wholly discontinued, execution may not issue without leave (*Ord.* 18, *r.* 2). Request for entry of judgment is usually by letter.

More often, discontinuance follows agreement between the parties and a letter to the court ends the matter. If doubt exists whether any agreement will be carried out, it is sometimes advisable to request the court to adjourn the proceedings *sine die*.

REFERENCES UNDER ORDER 19
Reference to arbitrator

The court has power, under s. 92 of the Act, to order proceedings to be referred to an arbitrator. *Order* 19, *r.* 1, applies. The procedure may be used in small claims by consumers acting without professional help.

An order may be made by a registrar if the sum claimed or amount involved does not exceed £75, or in any other case with the consent of the parties. An order may not be made *referring* proceedings *to a judge* without leave of the judge; or *to an outside arbitrator* except with the consent of the parties. If the court is satisfied that a *charge of fraud* against a party is in issue, an order may not be made except with the consent of that party.

An application may be made—

(a) on notice under *Ord*. 13, *r.* 1 (*"Form* Ex. 23 procedure"); or

(b) by the plaintiff in his particulars of claim; or

(c) by the defendant in his defence or counterclaim (there is a question printed on the prescribed *Form* 18 for this purpose).

In the case of an application under *Ord*. 13, *r.* 1, a fee of 50p is payable. In the other two cases, an order would be made on the return day or pre-trial review.

Order is in *Form* 111.

In the case of an outside arbitrator, the order is served on him as well as on the parties, but it will not be served at all until each party has paid into court the sum determined by the registrar in respect of the arbitrator's remuneration.

The reference is conducted under *Ord*. 19, *r*. 2(3)(*a*) to (*e*), with necessary modifications. *Ord*. 37, *r*. 7, applies to any application to set aside any award.

Directions to be given as to conduct of arbitration

The registrar should, in settling the terms on which an order of reference is to be made, consider the desirability of including such of the terms mentioned in the schedule below as he may think appropriate. The list is not exhaustive. The registrar may consider other terms to be desirable in the circumstances of the particular case. The parties should be given sufficient notice of a contemplated departure from the terms set out in the schedule to enable them to make any representations they may think fit. A party who wishes to propose a different term should inform the registrar and the other side before the order is made (*Practice Direction*, 21st September 1973, [1973] 3 All E.R. 448). When a party wishes to propose a different term, if it is of substance, presumably he should give notice in writing, either by letter, or in the notice of application.

Schedule.

1. The strict rules of evidence shall not apply in relation to the arbitration.
2. With the consent of the parties the arbitrator may decide the case on the basis of the statements and documents submitted by the parties. Otherwise, he should fix a date for the hearing.
3. Any hearing shall be informal and may be held in private.
4. At the hearing the arbitrator may adopt any method of procedure which he may consider to be convenient and to afford a fair and equal opportunity to each party to present his case.
5. If any party does not appear at the arbitration, the arbitrator may make an award on hearing any other party to the proceedings who may be present.
6. With the consent of the parties and at any time before giving his decision and either before or after the hearing, the arbitrator may consult any expert or call for an expert on any matter in dispute or invite an expert to attend the hearing as assessor.
7. The costs of the action up to and including the entry of

judgment shall be in the discretion of the arbitrator to be exercised in the same manner as the discretion of the court under the provisions of the County Court Rules (or as the case may be).

Reference for inquiry and report

The judge has power, under s. 93 of the Act, to refer to the registrar or a referee *for inquiry and report:*—

(*a*) any proceedings which require any prolonged examination of documents or any scientific or local investigation which cannot, in the opinion of the judge, conveniently be made before him;

(*b*) any proceedings where the question in dispute consists wholly or in part of matters of account;

(*c*) with the consent of the parties, any other proceedings;

(*d*) subject to any right to have particular cases tried with a jury, any question arising in any proceedings.

A registrar may make an order referring any question to a referee for inquiry and report if the sum claimed or amount involved does not exceed £75, in or any other case with the consent of the parties (*Ord.* 19, *r.* 2(2A)).

An application for an order may be made—

(*a*) on notice by any party before the hearing, such as under *Ord.* 13, *r.* 1; or

(*b*) by any party at the hearing; or

(*c*) at any stage of the proceedings by the court of its own motion.

In the case of an application under *Ord.* 13, *r.* 1, a fee of 50p is payable. *Ord.* 19, *r.* 2, applies. The order is in *Form* 112.

Actions where work done by builders is in dispute are sometimes referred under this section

Reference to European Court

An order referring a question to the European Court may be made by the judge before or at the trial or hearing of any action or matter either of his own motion or on the application of any party. When an order has been made, the registrar sends a copy of it to the Senior Master of the Supreme Court, Queen's Bench Division, for transmission to the registrar of the European Court. A registrar may not make an order. *Ord.* 19, *r.* 3, applies. For form of order, see R.S.C., *Appendix* A, *Form* 109.

ACCOUNTS AND INQUIRIES IN EQUITY PROCEEDINGS

A judgment or order directing accounts to be taken or inquiries to be made in equity proceedings, such as in the case of foreclosure proceedings, is in one of *Forms* 230 to 235. Forms of notice and of the registrar's certificate are in *Forms* 236 to 241. *Order* 29 applies.

EVIDENCE (*Ord.* 20)

Affidavits

Evidence in support of or in opposition to a petition may be by affidavit unless the judge otherwise directs (*Ord.* 20, *r.* 3).

The judge or registrar may at any time order that—

(*a*) any facts may be proved by affidavit; or

(*b*) the affidavit of a witness be read at the hearing on conditions as he thinks reasonable; or

(*c*) any witness whose attendance in court ought for some sufficient cause to be dispensed with be examined by interrogatories or before an examiner (*Ord.* 20, *r.* 4).

Where a party desires to use at the hearing an affidavit without an order, he may, not less than five clear days before the hearing, give notice, accompanied by a copy of the affidavit, to the party against whom it is to be used. Unless this party, not less than two clear days before the hearing, gives notice to the other party that he objects to the use of the affidavit, he is to be taken to have consented to the use of it (*Ord.* 20, *r.* 5 (1)).

In an ordinary action, if a defendant has not delivered a defence within the time limited, evidence by affidavit is admissible without notice, unless the court otherwise orders (*Ord.* 20, *r.* 5 (2)). Affidavits are commonly used under this rule in batches of debt-collecting actions.

In mortgage actions for possession, evidence in support or in opposition may be given by affidavit (*Ord.* 46, *r.* 21), but oral evidence is accepted. The practice of the Chancery Division, whereby the affidavit in support must be indorsed with a notice of appointment and a certificate of service of a copy, is not followed in county courts. *Order* 20, *r.* 5, applies.

Civil Evidence Act, 1968

Pleading conviction, finding of adultery or adjudication of paternity.—*Order* 20, *r.* 7A, applies. Any party who intends to adduce evidence of these in reliance on ss. 11 and 12 of the Civil Evidence Act, 1968, must include a statement of his intention with particulars in his particulars of claim or defence. If a defendant denies the conviction, finding or adjudication, or alleges it is erroneous, he must say so in his defence.

Hearsay evidence.—*Order* 20, *rr.* 20 to 30, apply. Where a party desires to give hearsay evidence which is admissible by virtue of ss. 2, 4 or 5 of the Civil Evidence Act, 1968, he must give notice of his desire to do so to the court and to every other party not less than fourteen clear days before the day fixed for trial or hearing, except where no defence is filed. See *County Court Practice* for details. R.S.C., *Ord.* 38, *rr.* 22 to 25, apply.

For forms, see E.F. Forms in the *Supreme Court Practice*, 1973, Vol. 2, paras. 502 *et seq.*

As to statements produced by a computer, the following specifically apply; ss. 5 and 6 (3) (*c*) of the 1968 Act, R.S.C., *Ord.* 38, *r.* 24, and *Form* EF4.

Witness summons (*Ord.* 20, *r.* 8)

Subpœnas in county court actions are called witness summonses.

Requirements on issue:—

    (*a*) Request or *præcipe* (*Form* 115) supplied by the court;
    (*b*) Plaint note or originating process;
    (*c*) *Fee*, 10p (No. 63); if service by bailiff, 50p in addition;
    (*d*) Conduct money (No. 63), if service by bailiff;
    (*e*) Stamped addressed envelope, if by post.

Conduct money must be sufficient to cover cost of travelling and, in addition, a sum for compensation for loss of time, namely, for professional persons, owners, directors or managers, of business, £4; police officers, £3; clerks, "artisans, labourers", and other persons , £1.50.

The summons may contain the name of one witness only, but as regards the name of the witness, it may be issued in blank. The summons and copy are drawn by the court; *Form* 113, to give oral evidence (*ad test.*), *Form* 114, to produce documents (*duces tecum*).

The summons must be served *personally* a reasonable time before the hearing. Affidavit of service is *Form* 116 (2) (supplied by the court). An affidavit of service is only required to enforce attendance. If service is by bailiff, it is advisable, in cases of doubt, to enquire at the court whether the summons has been served, as service may be close to the day of hearing. Notice of non-service should be sent (*Ord.* 8, *r.* 2 (*d*)).

Other matters

Notice to admit facts is in *Form* 117, admission of facts, *Form* 118, notice to inspect and admit, *Form* 119 and notice to produce documents, *Form* 120. These forms are not supplied by the court. *Order* 20, *rr.* 9 to 11, apply.

As to examination of witness out of court, *Ord.* 20, *r.* 18 applies.

For examination of witnesses abroad, s. 85 of the Act applies. Application is by originating summons to a master of the Queen's Bench Division in the High Court; R.S.C.. *Ord.* 107, *r.* 3, applies.

REGISTRAR'S COURTS

Additional courts, known as "registrar's courts", may be held when the judge is not sitting (s. 36 of the Act and *Ord.* 22). They are frequently held in vacation and in some small county courts where there is not sufficient work for the judge for more than the regular sitting.

The plaint note (*Form* 15), summons (*Form* 19) and notice of hearing in default action (*Form* 27 (2)), inform the parties what to do if they object to the hearing by the registrar. Objections are rare.

Where—

(a) the claim exceeds £75 and is disputed; or
(b) the claim is disputed and any party objects to the action being heard by the registrar; or
(c) an order is made for trial by jury; or
(d) any defendant files a third party notice or sets up a counterclaim exceeding £75;

the registrar, unless he has jurisdiction by leave of the judge and consent of the parties, must adjourn the action to a day when the judge is sitting (*Ord.* 22, *r.* 6).

HEARING AND JUDGMENTS AND ORDERS

Hearing before registrar

The registrar has power to hear and determine—

(a) by leave of the judge and in absence of objection by the parties, any action or matter where the amount involved does not exceed £75, or, in an action for return of goods, where the value or unpaid hire-purchase price does not exceed £75;
(b) by leave of the judge and with the consent of the parties, any other action or matter. However, this does not allow the registrar to hear a case where the jurisdiction is conferred on the judge alone (*Ord.* 23, *r.* 1).

If the defendant does not appear, or appears and admits the claim, the registrar has power to give judgment, with leave of the judge, whatever the cause of action and notwithstanding that the sum claimed or the amount involved exceeds £75 (*Ord.* 23, *rr.* 4 and 5).

Where plaintiff does not attend

If the plaintiff does not appear, or does not attend by affidavit, the proceedings are struck out. If the defendant attends and does not admit the claim, costs may be awarded against the plaintiff. The order is in *Form* 128 (*Ord.* 23, *r.* 2).

The action may be reinstated or restored for hearing. An application to reinstate the action may be made on the same or any subsequent day. An application made *ex parte* by letter may be accepted, but, in cases of dispute, an application should be made on notice in *Form* Ex. 23. *Fee:* if application is not made on day when action struck out, 50p.

Interest on damages

Where judgment is given for a sum which exceeds £200 and includes damages in respect of personal injuries, or in respect of a person's death, the court must include in that sum interest on those damages or on such part of them as the court considers appropriate, unless the court is satisfied that there are special reasons why no interest should be given (Law Reform (Miscellaneous Provisions) Act, 1934, s. 3, as amended by the Administration of Justice Act, 1969, s. 22).

The principles to be applied when awarding damages in personal injury actions were considered in *Jefford* v. *Gee* [1970] 1 All E.R. 1202.

Special damages.—Interest should be awarded from the date of the accident to the date of trial at *half* the appropriate rate.

Loss of future earnings.—No interest should be allowed.

Pain and suffering and loss of amenities; damages under the Fatal Accidents Acts; for loss of expectation of life under Law Reform (Miscellaneous Provision) Act, 1934.—Interest should be awarded at the appropriate rate from the date of service of the summons to the date of trial.

Appropriate rate.—The rate of interest should be that allowed by the court on the short-term investment account, taken as an average over the period for which the interest is awarded. The rates are as follows:

From 1st October, 1965, 5 per cent.;

From 1st September, 1966, $5\frac{1}{2}$ per cent.;

From 1st March, 1968, 6 per cent.;

From 1st March, 1969, $6\frac{1}{2}$ per cent.;

From 1st March, 1970, 7 per cent.;

From 1st April, 1971, $7\frac{1}{2}$ per cent.;

From 1st March 1973, 8 per cent.

The judgment should state the rate of interest and the period for which it is awarded and should state it as a gross sum without deducting tax.

In determining whether the county court has jurisdiction under the County Courts Act, 1959, by virtue of the amount claimed or awarded, no account is taken of the interest awarded (s. 3 (1c) of the Law Reform (Miscellaneous Provisions) Act, 1934).

Judgments and orders

The court draws up the judgment or order (*Ord*. 24, *r*. 8).

The court may order a sum of money to be paid in one sum or by instalments (s. 99 of the County Courts Act, 1959). If no day is specified for payment, then payment is to be made usually within fourteen days (*Ord*. 24, *r*. 13).

In a judgment for recovery of land, if no day is named for giving possession, a warrant may be issued after fourteen days (*Ord*. 25, *r*. 72). In the absence of a statutory power such as under the Rent Act 1968, the maximum time for possession should normally be four to five weeks (see *Sheffield Corporation* v. *Luxford* [1929] 2 K.B. 180). In the case of forfeiture for non-payment of rent, the time for giving possession must be not less than four weeks (s. 191 of the 1959 Act).

In the case of an *order enforceable by attachment*, the registrar must, if the order is in the nature of an injunction, at the time the order is drawn up, and in any other case on the application of the party for whose benefit the order is made, issue a copy of the order indorsed with a notice in *Form* 140 (penal notice) (with copy for endorsement or exhibit) to be served on the party liable personally (*Ord*. 25, *r*. 68). An order for substituted service may be made under *Ord*. 8, *r*. 6. Consideration should be given as to whether the judgment or order should also be served by post in case a party decides not to proceed by attachment when personal service cannot be effected.

A judgment or order *in the nature of a decree* is prepared by the registrar. The draft should be sent by him to such party as he thinks fit with an appointment to settle. Notice of the appointment, together with a copy of the draft, is served by the party, to whom the draft has been sent, on the other parties not less than one clear day before the day of the appointment. The registrar settles the draft in the presence of such parties that attend. Any money payable under such a judgment or order is payable forthwith unless the court otherwise orders (*Ord.* 24, *r.* 5). However, it seems to be the usual practice for the court to send copies of the draft to all parties (without an appointment) for their approval, or comments. If the draft cannot be agreed, an appointment is then given. In some courts, a party is requested first to submit the draft.

Drawing up of judgment.—Subject to any Act or other rule, no order giving leave to take any proceedings and no inter-locutory order need be drawn up or served, unless the court otherwise orders (*Ord.* 24, *r.* 7).

The general rule is that every judgment or order is, unless the court otherwise requires, prepared and served by the registrar and it is not necessary for the party, in whose favour the judgment or order is made, to prove that it reached the party to be served (*Ord.* 24, *r.* 8). This is the case with money judgments. Except where otherwise provided, a judgment or order may be served by ordinary post, and even though a party to be served is acting by solicitor, service may, if the registrar thinks fit, be effected on the party himself (*Ord.* 24, *r.* 8 (3)).

Copies and certificates of judgment

Copies or duplicates of a judgment or order are supplied by the court to any of the parties on payment of *fee* of 15p (No. 68(ii)). The fee is not usually charged for a defendant who is making a payment.

Certificates of judgment are supplied on payment of *fee* of 5p (No. 68(i)). They are usually required for an appeal, for issuing a bankruptcy notice and bankruptcy proceedings, and for garnishee proceedings. In these cases the full certificate in *Form* 141 (1) should be used. When a certificate of judgment is required for exhibiting to a *proof in bankruptcy*, the shortened form, *Form* 141 (3), is used. The certificate in *Form* 141 (2) is used when an action is transferred to another court to issue a judgment summons under *Ord.* 25, *r.* 48, or an application for an attachment of earnings order under *Ord.* 25, *r.* 79 (4).

A certificate of judgment is applied for by letter which must state the reason for which it is required.

Where the person applying for a certificate of judgment is not a party, he must state in writing, with particulars, the purpose for which he requires it, and the capacity in which he applies, and he must satisfy the registrar that the application may properly be granted. The registrar may refer the application to the judge (*Ord.* 24, *r.* 12).

Registration of judgments (*Register of County Court Judgments Regulations*, 1936)

Every *judgment* (not an *order*) for £10 or more (including costs) is registered, if it is not satisfied or complied with wholly or if £10 or more is still owing, at the expiration of one month from the date of judgment; or, if costs are to be taxed, then the time is reckoned from the date of taxation.

Every judgment or order in *Admiralty or equity proceedings* is registered within ten days after entry of the judgment or order.

The registry is kept by the Registrar of County Court Judgments, 140 Gower Street, London WC1E 6HT, where searches may be made. *Fees* (No. 72): search by person who attends, for every name, 10p; if by post, for entries against a named person, 25p, and in addition for every year more than three to which the search is to extend, 5p, and for every entry more than one, 5p; and for serial list, for every fifty entries copied and supplied, £3. An uncertified copy of any entry will be sent. If a certified copy of an entry is required, the fee is 25p.

Where a judgment has been set aside or reversed, the county court sends a certificate to that effect to the registry to cancel any entry, if it has been registered.

If a person wishes to have the registration of a judgment cancelled because the judgment has been satisfied, the party makes a request in writing to the registrar of the county court and on payment of a *fee* of 10p the court sends a certificate of satisfaction to the registry. Any money that has been paid direct to a plaintiff is usually required to be "passed through" by the plaintiff, or an affidavit from a judgment debtor may be accepted as proof of payment (*reg.* 6).

PAYMENT AFTER JUDGMENT

Moneys payable under a judgment or order must be paid into court except that, if an instalment order is not made, the court may direct that the money be paid by one party direct to another or his solicitor (s. 99 (3) of the Act). Under a judgment for possession of land, which is suspended on payment of rent, all instalments are usually ordered to be paid to the plaintiff or his agent.

Money paid *before* judgment direct to a plaintiff is credited in the judgment. Money paid *after* judgment direct to a party can be passed through the court books by completing a gummed receipt slip, supplied by the court, and marked "Pass", or some suitable wording.

County courts now remit moneys paid into court by payable order to judgment creditors or their solicitors without demand. Remittances are usually sent weekly on Thursdays or Fridays.

The court has jurisdiction to recall money paid out of court in error (*Gainsborough Mixed Concrete, Ltd.* v. *Duplex Petrol Installations, Ltd.* [1968] 3 All E.R. 267).

SUSPENSION AND VARIATION OF JUDGMENTS AND NEW ORDERS

Applications to suspend or vary a judgment or order, or to stay execution, and also for a new order, can be made under various Acts and rules. A "new order" supersedes the judgment. Most applications are made by defendants acting in person.

Requirements:

By judgment debtor:

    Two forms of application in *Form* Ex. 23 or Ex. 23A; unless to suspend a committal order under the Debtors

Act, 1869, in which case a request by letter or made orally on attendance at the court office is sufficient and *Ord.* 25, *r.* 54 (4), then applies and notices in *Forms* 387 and 388 are sent.

Order 24, *r.* 18, is one of the rules that applies.

When the application is made by a defendant in person, it is common practice for the court to send notice to the plaintiff or his solicitor. No fee.

By judgment creditor:

    (*a*) *Ex parte*, application in *Form* 143; for an order under *Ord.* 24, *r.* 17, to pay by instalments, or, if instalments already ordered, by the same or smaller instalments;

    (*b*) Plaint note or originating process;

    (*c*) *Fee*, 25p (No. 11);

    (*d*) Stamped addressed envelope, if by post.

Form 143 is supplied by the court.

Or, *if on notice:*

    (*a*) Two forms of application in *Form* Ex. 23;

    (*b*) Plaint note or originating process;

    (*c*) *Fee*, 25p, under *Ord.* 24, *r.* 19 (No. 11);

    (*d*) Stamped addressed envelope, if by post.

The judgment creditor usually serves by ordinary post, but in some courts, the court serves by post.

Forms of order: for new order under *Ord.* 24, *rr.* 17, 18 and 19, *Form* 144; for order to suspend or stay judgment, order execution or order of commitment or order for discharge of a debtor, *Form* 145.

The court may suspend or stay, on such terms as it thinks fit, any judgment or order (s. 99 (2) of the Act) and any execution (s. 123 of the Act), if it appears that a party is unable to pay any sum recovered against him. Where a warrant has been sent to another court for execution, the judge of that court has a similar power to suspend or stay the warrant (s. 138 (3) of the Act).

The judge has power to suspend an order of commitment under s. 160 of the Act where the debtor is unable to pay any sum, with terms as to the debtor's liability for re-arrest. The judge of a court to which the order has been sent for execution has similar powers in the case of the Debtors Act, 1869 (s. 161(5) of the Act). *Order* 25, *r*. 62A, applies. A registrar has power to suspend under *Ord*. 25, *r*. 8, with leave of the judge—see below.

Order 24, *r*. 13 (2)—a *judgment creditor* may apply on notice for an order for payment at an earlier date, if an order to pay by instalments is not made.

Order 24, *r*. 17—a *judgment creditor* may apply *ex parte* on a *præcipe* in *Form* 143, for payment by instalments, or if payment by instalments has already been ordered, either by the *same or smaller* instalments. If there has been no payment within six years, the registrar should refer the application to the judge.

Order 24, *r*. 18—a *judgment debtor* may apply on notice for further time to pay or to reduce the amount of the instalments payable by him.

Order 24, *r*. 19—a *judgment creditor* may apply on notice for an order that the amount unpaid be paid in one sum or by *larger* instalments than those previously ordered.

Order 24, *r*. 20—an application under *Ord*. 24, *rr*. 13, 18 or 19, above, should be made to the judge if the original order was made by him, and in any other case, to the registrar.

However, *Ord*. 25, *r*. 8—the registrar has power (with leave of the judge, usually granted) to suspend or stay any judgment or order of his court and to stay execution of any warrant issued by his court or sent to his court for execution. This power, apparently, includes power to suspend an order of commitment.

Order 25, *r*. 43 (4) and (5), applies for revoking an order made under the *Form* 179 procedure and the discharge of a debtor.

Order 37, *r*. 1 (4), applies as to stay of execution pending a new trial.

The Supreme Court Rules (R.S.C., *Ord*. 59, *r*. 13), apply in the case of stay of execution pending an appeal to the Court of Appeal, but application may be made also in the county court for a stay.

As to stay of an order for *possession of land* the court has power to stay or suspend execution of an order for possession—

(*a*) of a protected or statutory tenancy under the Rent Act, 1968, s. 11;

(*b*) of agricultural tied cottage under the Rent Act, 1965, s. 33;

(*c*) of a mortgaged dwelling-house under the Administration of Justice Act, 1970, s. 36, and the Administration of Justice Act, 1973, s. 8;

(*d*) for forfeiture for non-payment of rent under the Administration of Justice Act, 1965, s. 23; and

(*e*) under its inherent jurisdiction, the court has a very limited power (see *Moore* v. *Registrar of Lambeth* [1969] 1 All E.R. 782, at p. 785). See also *McPhail* v. *persons unknown* [1973] 3 All E.R. 393.

Hire purchase.—The court has power to stay, suspend or vary, judgments and warrants for delivery of goods under the Hire-Purchase Act, 1965, under s. 39. *Order* 46, *r.* 10 (4), applies.

EXAMINATION OF JUDGMENT DEBTOR

A judgment creditor may apply *ex parte* in *Form* 149 for an order that the debtor, or, if the debtor is a corporation, any officer thereof, be orally examined as to the debtor's means (*Ord.* 25, *r.* 2(1)). The examination may be ordered to take place before an officer of the court.

Requirements:

(*a*) Application in *Form* 149 (not supplied by the court);

(*b*) Plaint note or originating process;

(*c*) *Fee:* 25p (No. 36); if service by bailiff, in addition, 50p (No. 4) and conduct money;

(*d*) Stamped addressed envelope, if by post.

The court draws the order in *Form* 150 incorporating *Form* 140 (penal notice). The amount of conduct money is usually noted on the face of the order.

Where the judgment debtor does not reside or carry on business within the district of the court, the judgment creditor must first apply *ex parte* under *Ord.* 25, *r.* 48, to transfer the proceedings to the court for the district in which the debtor resides or carries on business. The application is made by letter as in attachment of earnings applications, stating the purpose of the transfer. *Fee:* 15p.

Before the registrar makes an order for oral examination, he may give the debtor an opportunity to file a statement or affidavit as to his means, usually within seven days (*Ord.* 25, *r.* 2(9)). A copy of any statement or affidavit filed is sent to the creditor, who may accept it in the place of an examination.

The order for oral examination must be served personally a reasonable time before the examination. Notice of service is not sent when service is by bailiff, but notice of non-service is sent. It is advisable to enquire at the court if service has been effected, in case there is a late return of non-service. If service is by solicitor, affidavit of service must be filed (*Form* 177 adapted). If the order is not served, the court should be informed as early as possible. When the order is not served, a new day will be fixed without fee. Rules as to substituted service apply.

Solicitor, agent or a solicitor's clerk attends to question the debtor. If the debtor does not attend, the examiner certifies to that effect. The order may be enforced by attachment. Costs are in the discretion of the registrar (see *Form* 150). The costs may be added to the judgment, or a separate order may be made for them. Costs may sometimes not be allowed unless the judgment creditor can show that the examination was justified (see Note in *Supreme Court Practice*, 1973, para. 48/1—3/8).

Costs allowable are:—

  Court fees;

  Conduct money;

  Solicitor's costs:—

    Lower Scale £1.00 (App. D, Part III);

    Higher Scale

Attendance to obtain order (Item 17)
>   Scales 1, 2 and 3: 50p;
>   Scale 4: 75p.

On examination without counsel (Item 10) for each
hour or part:—
>   Scale 1: £1.50;
>   Scale 2: £2;
>   Scale 3: £3;
>   Scale 4: £3 to £4.

If service by solicitor, Item 18 applies.

In *matrimonial proceedings*, an application for the oral
examination of a debtor is made to such divorce county court
as in the opinion of the applicant is nearest to the place where
the debtor resides or carries on business. An affidavit is
required and also a copy of the order if the application is
made in another court. M.C.R. *r.* 86(6) applies.

When an order for oral examination is made in the *High
Court*, the examination may be ordered to take place in a
county court (R.S.C., *Ord.* 48, *r.* 1(1)).

ENFORCEMENT OF AWARD OF TRIBUNAL

Order 25, *r.* 7A, applies.

Where, by any Act or statutory instrument other than the
County Court Rules, a sum of money may be recoverable as if
it were an order of the county court, an originating application
may be made for such an order.

Requirements:
>   (*a*) Originating application in *Form* 23;
>   (*b*) *Fee* (No. 2 (ii)): 5p for every £2 or part thereof in
>   respect of which the application is made; minimum,
>   50p; maximum, £3.

Unless otherwise provided,
>   (*a*) the application is filed in the court for the district in
>   which the person by whom the sum is payable resides
>   or carries on business;
>   (*b*) it is made *ex parte*;
>   (*c*) it is heard by the registrar;

(*d*) at the hearing the applicant must produce the original award, order or agreement under which the sum is payable, or a duplicate of it; and

(*e*) he must file a copy of it together with an affidavit verifying the amount remaining due.

No form of affidavit is prescribed, but *Form* 175 may be adapted. The order is in *Form* 165.

The order may be enforced by execution or attachment of earnings. It may also be enforced by a charging order on the debtor's land (s. 141 (4) of the Act).

An originating application may be issued in respect of an order for costs under the Redundancy Payments Act, 1965, s. 46, and for money awarded under the Industrial Tribunals (Selective Employment Payments) Regulations, 1966. For other Acts, see notes to *Ord.* 25, *r.* 7A, in the *County Court Practice.* Such an application may be issued in respect of compensation awarded by an industrial tribunal (Industrial Relations Act, 1971, Sched. 6, para. 10.)

ENFORCEMENT BY EXECUTION
Warrant of Execution against goods

Requirements for issue of warrant of execution:

(*a*) Request or *præcipe* (*Form* 158) (supplied by the court);

(*b*) Plaint note or originating process;

(*c*) *Fee* (No. 38 (i)): for every £2 or part thereof, 25p, minimum, 75p, maximum, £10;

(*d*) Stamped addressed envelope, if by post;

(*e*) If judgment debtor is a "farmer", an official certificate of result of search, dated not more than three days beforehand, under Agricultural Credits Act, 1928 (15p added to warrant);

In addition, if judgment or order other than of a county court:—

(*f*) Office copy of judgment or order, or other appropriate evidence;

(*g*) Affidavit in support (*Form* 175) (supplied by the court);

(*h*) Copy of the sheriff's return, if any.

(*Order*. 25, *rr*. 13 and 13A).

Solicitor's costs added to warrant: 50p if issued for sum exceeding £20 and up to £500; and 75p for sums exceeding £500 (Item 17 or 23) (*Ord*. 25, *r*. 24 (2)).

When the execution is on a judgment or order of the High Court, the warrant is issued in the court in the district of which the execution is to be levied. Notice of issue in *Form* 180A is sent by the court to the proper officer of the High Court.

A warrant may be issued for the whole balance when a judgment debtor is in default. Where an order has been made for payment by instalments, it may be issued for part, but it must be issued for not less than £3, or the amount of one monthly instalment or four weekly instalments, as the case may be, whichever is the greater; provided that no warrant may be issued unless at the time when it is issued the whole or part of an instalment which has already become due remains unpaid and any earlier warrant has expired or been satisfied or abandoned. (*Ord*. 25, *r*. 13 (5)). The judgment creditor indicates on the *præcipe* the amount for which he requests a "part" warrant to issue. Where a "part" warrant is issued, the registrar of the court, where the warrant is to be executed, may direct that a notice in *Form* 160A be sent to the judgment debtor allowing him seven days in which to satisfy the warrant (*Ord*. 25, *r*. 13 (6)).

The court marks the number of the warrant and fee on the plaint note or originating process. Where warrants are issued by solicitors or plaintiffs in large numbers, some county courts dispense with the production of plaint notes and will mark the warrant numbers and fees on a list prepared by the party issuing.

If the warrant is to issue against one only of two or more judgment debtors, this must be shown clearly on the *præcipe*.

Where the name of a party differs from the name as it appeared in the judgment, and the judgment creditor satisfies the registrar that the amended name is applicable to the person as stated in the judgment, both names must be inserted in the warrant as follows: "*C.D.* sued as [*or* suing as] *A.D.*"

(*Ord.* 25, *r.* 13 (2)). If the debtor's name is clearly that of the original debtor, such as, when the full names are given instead of initials, or additional initials are given, the *præcipe* is accepted as sufficient. If there is any doubt, an accompanying letter of explanation is accepted, which can be referred to the registrar personally. The registrar may require an application to be made on notice to amend the debtor's name (no fee).

Leave is required to issue a warrant of execution after the expiration of two years from the date of the judgment or order, or from the date of some payment thereunder. Where leave is given, a note thereof is made on the warrant (*Ord.* 25, *r.* 16). Application for leave is usually first made *ex parte* in writing on the face of the *præcipe* (no fee).

Leave is also required where there is an attachment of earnings order in force (Attachment of Earnings Act, 1971, s. 8 (2) (*b*)).

Leave of the judge is required, where a judgment summons is pending or an order of commitment is outstanding (*Ord.* 25, *r.* 17). Application can be made *ex parte*, but notice to the debtor would be normal (no fee).

Against a firm.—Where a judgment or order is against a firm, execution may issue as follows:—

    (*a*) against the property of the partnership;

    (*b*) against any person who had admitted in the action or matter that he was a partner when the cause of action arose, or who has been adjudged to be liable as a partner;

    (*c*) against any person who was individually served with the summons as a partner or a person sought to be made liable—

        (i) if the action is a default action and judgment was entered in default of defence; or

        (ii) if there was a trial and the person so served failed to appear at the trial

(*Order.* 25, *r.* 18 (2)).

The court official refers to the court file to confirm the

position when a judgment creditor wishes to issue against a partner in the above circumstances.

If the party who has obtained the judgment or order claims to be entitled to issue execution against any other person as a partner, he may apply to the court for leave to do so and the following provisions apply:—

    (a) he must give to the alleged partner not less than three clear days' notice of his application;

    (b) the notice must be served personally;

    (c) on the hearing of the application, the court may order the questions of liability to be tried as an issue, if liability is disputed

(*Order.* 25, *r.* 18 (2)).

    Requirements:

    (a) Application in *Form* Ex. 23 and copy for service;

    (b) No fee, except if for service by bailiff, 50p.

The application must show the address for service and the address of the judgment creditor or his solicitor. The application is heard by the registrar.

Duration.—A warrant of execution remains in force, if unexecuted, for one year from and exclusive of the day of issue, but it may, before its expiration, be renewed by leave of the court for one year, and so on from time to time during its currency. A note of the renewal is indorsed on the warrant which retains its priority (*Ord.* 25, *r.* 14).

Application for renewal is usually made *ex parte* by letter, which sets out the circumstances and reason for delay. No fee. If a warrant has expired, its costs are added to any subsequent warrant.

Levy.—If the place of levy is not within the district of the court, the warrant is sent to the court in the district of which levy is to be made. That court, known as the "foreign" court, adds its local number to the warrant. The local number appears in notices sent by the "foreign" court.

When a warrant is sent to a "foreign" court its priority is taken from the time of its receipt there, and not from the

G

time of making an application for its issue at the "home" court (Administration of Justice Act, 1965, s. 22 (1)).

If a warrant has not been executed within one month (or, in the case of a warrant exceeding £20, within fourteen days) from the date of issue or receipt, the registrar sends notice in *Form* 157 to the execution creditor, and also to the "home" court if the warrant has been received from another court (*Ord.* 25, *r.* 10).

When the warrant has been sent to another court for levy any inquiry should be made there. If the inquiry is made by letter, the number of the warrant should be quoted as well as the plaint number. The local number should also be quoted, if known; otherwise an indication should be given as to when it was sent to that other court. A stamped addressed envelope should be enclosed for any reply.

The warrant is handed to a bailiff, who is an official of the county court, for execution. If he intends to levy, he gives the execution debtor, or leaves at the place of levy, a notice of levy in *Form* 162, or 162A, B or C, as appropriate. The notice informs the debtor of the amount required and that, if the amount is paid within half an hour, no more costs will be incurred. The notice sets out the fees which become payable and the circumstances under which the goods levied upon will be removed and sold.

A general levy is first made. If payment is likely to be made, the bailiff may allow a reasonable time for payment and no further fees are payable. If the furniture, any motor vehicle, or other goods are subject to a hire purchase agreement, the bailiff asks for evidence, such as to see the agreement itself. If a claim is made to the goods by some other person, such as a wife, a claim in writing is taken, unless it is obvious that the goods do not belong to the debtor. If the goods are saleable, the bailiff usually takes walking possession. For a description of walking possession, see *Lloyds, etc., Ltd.* v. *Modern Cars, etc., Ltd.* [1964] 2 All E.R. 732. For effect of walking possession, as regards third persons, see *Abingdon R.D.C.* v, *O'Gorman* [1968] 3 All E.R. 79.

As to caravans and houseboats, there appears to be no

authoritative decision to say whether they may be seized under a warrant of execution whilst used as a dwelling or intermittently as a dwelling, or when they are fixed to the land. If a registrar or bailiff refused to levy, a complaint might be made by way of an application to the judge under s. 164 of the Act. An order might be made for the trial of the issue. Note *Lloyds, etc., Ltd.* v. *Modern Cars, etc., Ltd.* (*supra*), where a caravan was levied upon.

Wearing apparel and bedding of the debtor and his family, and the tools and implements of his trade, to the value of £50 are excepted from levy (s. 124 of the Act and S.I. 1963 No. 1297).

No possession fee is payable in the case of walking possession until the goods are removed. No appraisement should be made until the expiration of at least three days after seizure unless the goods are of a perishable nature or are sold at the request in writing of the execution debtor before that time. or are removed (*Ord.* 25, *r.* 27). The appraisement is usually made (after removal) by the auctioneer who acts as broker for the court.

When the goods are removed, the bailiff gives to the execution debtor an inventory in *Form* 166. Notice of sale in *Form* 167 must be given to the debtor at least twenty-four hours before the time fixed for the sale (*Ord.* 25, *r.* 28).

The fees payable on a levy for possession, removal and sale are Nos. 39 to 43 in the County Court Fees Order, 1971, and are set out in the notice of levy left with the execution debtor.

If a sale does not realise sufficient to cover the costs of levy, the execution creditor may be required to pay the deficiency (*County Court Fees Order*, 1971, *Art.* 3 (3)).

Warrants of execution may be issued concurrently for execution in one or more districts, but the costs of more than one warrant may not be allowed against the execution debtor except by order of the court (*Ord.* 25, *r.* 23). Only one fee for issue is payable.

Costs of warrants, whether executed or unproductive, are allowed against the execution debtor (*Ord.* 25, *r.* 24). If they are not recovered under execution, they may not be included in a judgment summons or new order or in an attachment of earnings order, nor may money paid into court be appropriated to such costs, until the rest of the debt and costs have been paid (*Ord.* 25, *rr.* 65 and 86 (2)). Money paid into court between the issue of a warrant of execution and its final return is usually treated as payment under the warrant. As to recovering unsatisfied costs of execution under garnishee proceedings, the practice varies. Unsatisfied costs are not usually included in an amount for which a bankruptcy notice issues, but it is understood that the costs may be included for proof in bankruptcy.

Suspension of warrant by judgment creditor.—Where an execution creditor requests the bailiff to withdraw from possession, he is deemed to have abandoned the execution and the registrar marks the warrant as *withdrawn* by request; but, if the request is made in consequence of a claim to the goods seized, the execution is deemed to be abandoned only in respect of the goods claimed. However, where the request indicates that it is in pursuance of an arrangement between the execution creditor and the execution debtor, the registrar marks the warrant as *suspended* by request of the execution creditor, and the execution creditor may subsequently have the warrant re-issued (*Ord.* 25, *r.* 25). The request to suspend a warrant by a judgment creditor is, in practice, given by letter.

If it is likely that goods have been removed or costs of possession incurred, the execution creditor may wish to ensure that he does not become liable for the costs.

A warrant sent to another court for execution may be returned to the home court after it is suspended if the judgment creditor is not prejudiced thereby. Notice in *Form* 154A is sent to the parties informing them of the return (*Ord.* 25, *r.* 11).

Re-issue.—A warrant suspended at the request of the execution creditor may be re-issued. If there has been possession of goods, there is a fee payable (No. 38 (ii)), 25p, which is added to the warrant. Priority is reckoned from the time of re-issue (*Ord.* 25, *r.* 25 (2)).

Otherwise, a warrant may be re-issued without fee, e.g.,

after a suspension by order of the court, and for a fresh address.
Requirements:

(a) *Præcipe* for execution (*Form* 158) marked "Re-issue",
or letter;

(b) Plaint note or originating process, so that fresh
warrant number may be marked thereon, should also
be produced.

When a warrant has been sent to another court and not
returned to the home court, the request should be made to
that other court, if the address is within the same district,
in which case it is usual to make the request by letter, quoting
the local number.

Payment.—If a warrant, being executed in the home court,
is paid, the usual rule as to notice of payment into court
applies. If the warrant has been sent to another court for
execution, that court remits the money to the home court and
at the same time sends notice to the execution creditor
(*Ord.* 25, *r.* 9 (2) (*a*)).

Where "under an execution in respect of a judgment for
a sum exceeding £20", goods are sold or money is paid in
order to avoid a sale, after deducting costs of executing the
warrant, the money is retained fourteen days under the
Bankruptcy Act, 1914, s. 41 (2), or the Companies Act, 1948,
s. 326 (2), and notice is sent to the execution creditor and
home court, if any, in *Form* 163. Money will be remitted
automatically after the expiration of the statutory period
from a "foreign" court to the home court.

The amount of £20 referred to is the amount of the warrant,
and not the judgment, plus all legal expenses incidental to
the levy. If money is paid to the home court, when a warrant
has been sent to another court for execution, the money
received at the home court is not retained (see Williams on
Bankruptcy).

Claim to goods taken in execution

Where a claim is made to the goods levied upon, the bailiff
obtains the claim in writing (*Ord.* 28, *r.* 1). Notice of the
claim is sent by the registrar in *Form* 213, and, except where

the claim is to the proceeds or value of the goods, a notice to the claimant in *Form* 214 (*Ord.* 28, *r.* 2).

If it is obvious that the claim is a good one, such as a lodger living in furnished rooms, a return of non-execution of *nulla bona* is usually sent. Where it is obvious that the execution creditor might wish to dispute the claim, the rule is strictly followed.

If *Form* 213 is not sent, but the court has made a return of non-execution and the execution creditor wishes to dispute the claim, he should instruct the court, normally by letter, that he wishes to dispute the claim, requesting the registrar to issue interpleader proceedings.

Where *Form* 213 is sent, if within four days of receiving the notice the execution creditor gives notice to the registrar that he admits the claim, or requests the registrar to withdraw from possession, he will only be liable to the registrar for possession fees or expenses incurred before the registrar receives the notice from the execution creditor (*Ord.* 23 *r.* 3 (1)). Usually, walking possession having been taken, and the goods not being removed until the question of admitting the claim is settled, there are no further costs.

As to claims by the landlord for rent, the procedure is set out in s. 137 of the Act.

Interpleader proceedings under execution.—If the execution creditor does not give notice admitting the claim or requesting the registrar to withdraw from possession within the four days, the registrar enters interpleader proceedings. Interpleader summonses to the execution creditor and claimant are prepared in *Forms* 215 to 218, usually *Forms* 215 and 216 (*Ord.* 28, *r.* 5). No fee.

In county court executions, a levy must be made before interpleader proceedings may be commenced.

The summonses must be served not less than fourteen clear days before the return day (normally by bailiff) in accordance with the rules for the service of ordinary summonses. No fee. Where the claimant has not made a deposit or given security in accordance with s. 135 of the Act, the summons may, if the registrar thinks fit, be served less than fourteen clear days before the return day (*Ord.* 28, *r.* 6). The summons to be served on the execution creditor is usually served on his solicitor, if one is acting for him, in anticipation that the solicitor has instructions to accept service.

As directed in the summons to him, the claimant must, within eight days of service upon him (inclusive of the day of service), or, if the time has been abridged, within reasonable time before the return day, file in the court office two copies of the particulars of any goods alleged to be his property and the ground of his claim, or, in the case of a claim for rent, particulars stating the amount thereof, and the period and the premises in respect of which the rent is claimed to be due. He must include in the particulars a statement of his full name, address and occupation. The registrar sends a copy of the particulars to the execution creditor. However, the judge may, if he thinks fit, hear the proceedings although no particulars have been filed (*Ord.* 28, *r.* 8).

The hearing takes place before the judge. The order is in one of the *Forms* 219 to 221. If the claimant does not appear at the hearing, he may be barred from prosecuting his claim (*cf.* R.S.C., *Ord.* 17, *r.* 5(3)). Note *J.R.P. Plastics* v. *Gordon Rossall Plastics* [1950] 1 All E.R. 241. The order must contain directions by whom any court fees are to be paid and how any money in court is to be applied (*Ord.* 28, *r.* 15). If the claim is barred the warrant is returned to the bailiff for the execution to be completed.

As to damages claimed by the claimant, *Ord.* 28, *rr.* 11 to 13, apply.

Warrant of attachment (*Ord.* 25, *rr.* 67 to 70)

An order in the nature of an injunction and all orders which, if they were in an action or matter in the High Court, could be enforced by attachment or committal, may be similarly enforced by order of the judge (*Ord.* 25, *r.* 67).

When an order enforceable by attachment has been made, if the order is for the oral examination of a judgment debtor or is in the nature of an injunction, or, in any other case, on the application of the party for whose benefit the order was made, a copy of the order indorsed with, or incorporating, a notice in *Form* 140 (penal notice) must be served on the respondent personally (*Ord.* 25, *r.* 68 (1)). A duplicate is issued for indorsement of service by the bailiff, or to exhibit to an affidavit of service.

Fee: for service by bailiff, 50p.

If the party served fails to obey the order, the registrar, on the application of the party entitled to enforce it, must issue a notice of application in *Form* 194 not less than two clear days after service of the indorsed copy of the order, unless the judge gives leave for the notice to be issued sooner. The notice must be served personally (*Ord.* 25, *r.* 68 (2) and (3)). The notice must be served at least one clear day before the hearing of the application (*Ord.* 13, *r.* 1). It should not normally be served so close to the hearing.

In some courts the notice is prepared by the court on a request in writing by letter; in other courts, the form of application and copy are drawn by the applicant. *Fees:* 50p (No. 49 (i)), if service by bailiff, 50p (No. 4). *Form* 194 is supplied by the court.

The application is to the judge. The order for the issue of the warrant is in *Form* 195, and the warrant is in *Form* 196. A copy of the order must be served on the respondent, either before, or at the time of, the execution of the warrant unless the judge otherwise orders. *Form* 195 may be served by post.

For committal against a director of a company, note *Biba, Ltd.* v. *Stratford Investment, Ltd.* [1972] 3 All E.R. 1041.

The warrant is issued at the request in writing of the applicant, usually by letter, but an adapted *præcipe* (*Form* 183) can be used. *Fee:* 50p (No. 49 (ii)).

As to enforcement by attachment of a solicitor's undertaking, *Ord.* 25, *r.* 69, applies.

A person arrested under a warrant of attachment is imprisoned until he purges his contempt. As to his discharge, *Ord.* 25, *r.* 70, applies.

Requirements:
(a) Application in *Form* Ex. 23 and copy for service on other party;
(b) Affidavit in support and copy for service.
No fee.

The application is "for an order that I be discharged from custody, I being desirous of purging my contempt".

If the order of attachment does not direct that the application be made to the judge, it may be made to the registrar.

The application must be served one clear day before the hearing.

The order of discharge is in *Form* 199.

Warrant of possession (*Ord.* 25, *rr.* 71 to 73)

A judgment or order for the recovery of land or for the delivery of possession of land, whether made in an action for the recovery of land, or in any other proceedings, may be enforced by warrant of possession (*Ord.* 25, *r.* 71 (1)).

Requirements:
(a) Request or *præcipe* in *Form* 158A (supplied by the court);
(b) Plaint note or originating process;
(c) *Fee:* for possession only, £2; where the warrant is to recover money in addition, £2, plus 20p for every £2 or part, but the total fee is not to exceed £5 (No. 47);
(d) Stamped addressed envelope, if by post.

The fee and warrant number are marked on the plaint note or originating process.

The *præcipe* incorporates a certificate to be signed by the plaintiff or his solicitor that the defendant is in default.

The warrant is in *Form* 200 or *Form* 401 (summary proceedings). Separate warrants may issue for possession and for any money judgment (*Ord.* 25, *r.* 73).

An appointment has to be made to meet the bailiff at the premises. The practice for obtaining an appointment varies between courts. Usually a bailiff makes a preliminary visit to prepare the party for giving possession, to see if there is likely to be resistance requiring the aid of the police, and to see if there are any children requiring the presence of a welfare officer from the local authority.

For the purpose of executing a warrant to give possession of any premises, it is not necessary to remove any goods or chattels from the premises (s. 147 of the Act). County court bailiffs, therefore, do not provide for the removal of the furniture on the premises. The plaintiff or his agent makes his own arrangement. Locks are sometimes changed to prevent the defendant re-entering.

A warrant of possession may be suspended on a request by the plaintiff in writing.

A warrant of possession remains in force for one year, but may be extended by leave of the court before its expiration and renewed for one year and so on from time to time during the currency of the renewed warrant (*Ord.* 25, *r.* 71A). Enquiry should be made at the court to determine the mode of making the application for leave.

If a bailiff discovers persons other than the defendant and his family living on the premises, he reports the matter to the registrar. The registrar may require information from the plaintiff similar to that which is required in the High Court under R.S.C., *Ord.* 45, *r.* 3 (3), and may require any person to be given an opportunity to apply similar to the proceeding under R.S.C., *Ord.* 15, *r.* 10; or he may determine that the warrant for possession is not sufficient to eject any person other than the defendant and his family. No affidavits are normally necessary. C.C.R., *Ord.* 15, *r.* 10, applies to proceedings before judgment.

If a defendant re-enters after being ejected under a warrant of possession, in the High Court, an order may be made for the issue of a writ of restitution (Form No. 68 in Appendix A to the R.S.C.). A similar procedure may be adopted for county court proceedings but there is no equivalent warrant of restitution in county courts. In such cases, an application (*Form Ex.* 23) by the plaintiff on notice to the defendant can be made for the re-issue of the warrant or for leave to issue a fresh warrant. No fee. No affidavit is necessary in the first instance.

Warrant of delivery

Order 25, *rr.* 74 to 76, applies.

There are three forms of warrant of delivery—

Form 203 —Warrant of delivery and execution for money judgment and costs (specific delivery);

Form 203A—Warrant of delivery and execution for money judgment and costs under the Hire-Purchase Act, 1965, s. 35 (4) (*b*) (specific delivery);

Form 204 —Warrant of delivery where, if goods are not returned, levy is to be made for their value, and execution for money judgment and costs (delivery of goods or their value).

Where the judgment or order does not give the defendant an option to retain the goods on payment of their value, the plaintiff applies for a warrant in *Form* 203 or 203A (specific delivery).

Where the judgment or order is for the delivery of goods or their value, then the plaintiff applies for a warrant in *Form* 204 (return of goods or value). If, instead, the plaintiff wishes to issue a warrant for specific delivery of goods without the option being given of paying the value, he must make a special application to do so (cf. R.S.C., *Ord.* 45, *r.* 4). Such applications are rare. If the defendant does not comply with the judgment or order to return the goods, the plaintiff may apply for leave to issue a warrant of execution for the amount of the value (*Metals & Ropes Co., Ltd.* v. *Tattersall* [1966] 3 All E.R. 401).

The plaintiff may have execution for any sum of money and costs by the warrant of delivery or by a separate warrant. A judgment or order for delivery of goods may be enforced by attachment (*Ord.* 25, *rr.* 74 (3) and 68 (1)).

Requirements:—

(*a*) Request or *præcipe* in *Form* 158B (supplied by the court);

(*b*) Plaint note or originating process;

(*c*) *Fee:* see below;

(*d*) Stamped addressed envelope, if by post;

(*e*) If judgment debtor is a "farmer", an official certificate, not dated more than three days beforehand, of result of search under Agricultural Credits Act, 1928 (15p added to warrant).

Fee (No. 48) : 25p for every £2 or part thereof of the value of the goods; maximum £5. The value is to be (*a*) if the goods were supplied under a hire-purchase agreement (when the plaint fee would have been taken under Fee No. 1 (v) (*a*)), the balance of the hire-purchase price attributable to the goods at the time when the warrant is issued; (*b*) otherwise, the value stated in the judgment, or if none so stated, the value on which the plaint fee was calculated. In every other case, the maximum fee is payable. However, where the warrant is for the recovery of a sum of money in addition to delivery, this sum is to be added to the value, and the fee is calculated on the total.

Solicitor's costs of 50p are added to warrant if the value of the goods plus the sum of money, if any, for which the warrant issues, exceeds £20, but, if in excess of £500, then 75p (Item 17 or 23). This practice seems to be generally accepted.

The rules which apply to warrants of execution against goods also apply to warrants of delivery, so far as applicable (*Ord*. 25, *r*. 75 (3)).

The goods, which are the subject of the warrant, are normally delivered to the plaintiff or his agent at the address where the goods are. The plaintiff has to supply labour and transport for their removal. The method of giving an appointment varies between courts and enquiry should be made on issue as to how an appointment will be given. A preliminary visit is usually made by the bailiff before an appointment is made.

JUDGMENT SUMMONS

Order 25, *rr*. 33 to 66, apply.

A judgment summons is issued pursuant to the Debtors Act, 1869, s. 5. The Administration of Justice Act, 1970, s. 11, provides that a judgment summons may be issued in a county court in respect of—

(*a*) a High Court or a county court maintenance order; or

(*b*) a judgment or order for the payment of any taxes, contributions or liabilities specified in Sched. 4 to the Act.

Schedule 4 specifies—

(*a*) Income tax or any other tax or liability recoverable under the Taxes Management Act, 1970, ss. 65, 66 or 68;

(*b*) Selective employment tax under the Finance Act, 1966, s. 44;

(*c*) Contributions under—

(i) National Insurance Act, 1965, s. 3 (flat-rate) or s. 4 (graduated);

(ii) National Health Service Contributions Act, 1965, s. 1;

(iii) National Insurance (Industrial Injuries) Act, 1965, s. 2;

(*d*) Redundancy Fund contributions under the Redundancy Payments Act, 1965, s. 27.

Requirements:

(*a*) Request or *præcipe* (*Form* 170);

(*b*) Plaint note or originating process;

(*c*) *Fee* (No. 50): 20p for every £2, or part thereof, maximum £3; plus, if service by bailiff, 50p for each defendant, unless service by post when certificate in *Form* 172 is filed;

(*d*) Conduct money, if any;

(*e*) Stamped addressed envelope, if by post;

(*f*) If judgment against a firm, affidavit in *Form* 174 and copy;

If on a judgment or order of a court other than a county court—

(*g*) Office copy of the judgment or order;

(*h*) Affidavit in *Form* 175; if against a firm, then affidavit in *Form* 174 and copy, with the necessary additional paragraphs;

(*i*) Copy of the sheriff's return to writ of execution, if any.

All forms are supplied by the court.

The number of the judgment summons is endorsed on the plaint note or originating process with the place, date and time of hearing.

When it is desired to issue a judgment summons against more than one partner in a firm, a separate summons must be issued for each partner (see note at foot of the form of judgment summons *Form* 173).

A judgment summons may be issued only in the court for the district in which the debtor resides or carries on business unless it is issued against joint debtors (*Order.* 25, *r.* 33).

Transfer of proceedings for a judgment summons (*Ord.* 25 *r.* 48).—Where a judgment creditor wishes to issue a judgment summons in another county court having jurisdiction to issue the summons, he may apply *ex parte* to transfer the proceedings to that court. The application is made by letter and should state the address of the judgment debtor. *Fee:* 15p (No. 52).

The court sends a certificate of judgment or order to that court and the registrar of the other court gives the proceedings a fresh plaint number and sends notice in *Form* 90A to both parties.

Service.—Unless a certificate in *Form* 172 is filed, a judgment summons must be served personally. Where a judgment summons is served personally, conduct money (minimum 5p) may be paid to the judgment debtor (*Ord.* 25, *r.* 39). A judgment summons may be served by post if a certificate in *Form* 172 is filed.

A judgment summons must be served not less than ten clear days before the day fixed for hearing. If service is otherwise than by the court, an affidavit of service (*Form* 177) must be filed.

If the court has been unable to serve a judgment summons, notice of non-service (*Form* 178) is sent by the court.

Successive judgment summons (Ord. 25, r. 41).—Where a judgment summons has not been served, successive judgment summonses may be issued within six months of the date of the original issue.

Application to re-issue a judgment summons, or to issue a successive judgment summons, may be made by letter, but is conveniently made on filing a fresh *præcipe*, suitably marked.

Fees: on the issue of a second or subsequent successive judgment summons 15p (No. 51); for service by bailiff after an amendment, 25p (No. 4).

Hearing of Judgment Summons.—Where a judgment summons has been served by post following a certificate for postal service in *Form* 172, no order of commitment may be made against the debtor unless (*a*) he appears at the hearing, or (*b*) the judge is satisfied that the summons came to his knowledge in sufficient time for him to appear at the hearing (*Ord. 25, r. 39*).

A judgment creditor may appear by affidavit if he does not reside or carry on business within the district of the court (*Ord. 25, r. 46*).

The judge has power to commit to prison for a term not exceeding six weeks (Debtors Act, 1869, s. 5).

If the judge is of opinion that an order of commitment ought not to be made, he may make a new order for payment of the balance owing. He may make an attachment of earnings order (Attachment of Earnings Act, 1971, s. 3 (4) and (6)). A new order is in *Form* 192, or, in the case of a firm, in *Form* 193.

If an order of commitment is made, it is usually suspended, on payment in one sum or by instalments. *Notice* of it is in *Form* 182 which is sent to the debtor by post.

Costs.—On the hearing of a judgment summons, no costs may be allowed unless—

    (*a*) the judge is satisfied that the debtor has had, since the date of the original judgment or order, the means to pay the sum in which default has been made; or

(*b*) the summons is on a judgment or order of another
court, or a court other than a county court;

provided that, where conduct money has been paid to the
debtor, and the debtor does not attend the hearing, the judge
may, if he thinks fit, allow it as costs (*Ord.* 25, *r.* 66).

Solicitors' costs allowed on the hearing are: for over £5
and up to £20, £1; for over £20 and up to £500, £2; for over
£500, £3.

Costs and fees of a "not served" judgment summons are
not usually asked for or allowed unless paid under the judgment summons.

Costs incurred on an execution, but not recovered thereunder, may not be included in a judgment summons or in a
new order (*Ord.* 25, *r.* 65).

Non-attendance at hearing.—If a debtor does not attend the
hearing, the judge may adjourn the summons to a specified
date and order the debtor to attend then. The rules prescribing
the procedure are in *Ord.* 25, *r.* 43. The form of order requiring
the debtor to attend is in *Form* 179, and, in consequence, the
procedure is known as the "179 procedure". The order com-
mitting the debtor to prison, or warrant, is in *Form* 179A. No
fees are payable. *Order* 25, *r.* 43, contains the procedure for
an application by a debtor for the revocation of the order,
or for his discharge. The order for revocation or discharge is
in *Form* 179B.

If a judgment summons is struck out for non-attendance of
the judgment creditor, or is adjourned generally, an application
may be made to restore it to the list for hearing. Application
is usually by letter. A fee of 50p is payable on an application
to restore after a judgment summons has been struck out
unless made on the same day.

Issue of order of commitment

If a debtor makes default, the order of commitment (or
warrant) may be issued at the request of the judgment creditor,

Requirements:

(a) Request or *præcipe* in *Form* 183 (supplied by the court);

(b) Plaint note or originating process;

(c) *Fee* (No. 53) 5p for every £ or part, minimum 50p, maximum £3;

(d) Stamped addressed envelope, if by post.

Where two or more debtors are ordered to be committed, a separate order of commitment (or warrant) must be issued for each debtor (*Ord.* 25, *r.* 56). If the orders are issued at the same time, only one fee is payable.

If the order (or warrant) is not executed within a month, notice of non-execution is given by the court in *Form* 157. If the debtor is arrested and conveyed to prison, there is no rule requiring the court to notify the judgment creditor. The creditor has to inquire as to the result. Payments recovered are notified in accordance with the usual rule as to payments into court.

Suspension of order of commitment

An order of commitment (or warrant) may be suspended by the judgment creditor after issue. A letter is normally addressed to the registrar for the purpose.

If a debtor wishes to apply for a suspension of an order of commitment, he may either attend at or write to, the court office, stating his reasons for his inability to comply with the order. The registrar fixes a day for hearing the application and sends notice in *Form* 387 to the judgment creditor and *Form* 388 to the judgment debtor giving three clear days' notice (*Ord.* 25, *r.* 54 (4)).

ATTACHMENT OF EARNINGS

The Attachment of Earnings Act, 1971, and *Ord.* 25, *rr.* 77 to 94, apply.

The High Court may make an attachment of earnings order to secure payments under a High Court maintenance order (s. 1 (1) of the 1971 Act).

H

A magistrates' court may make an attachment of earnings order to secure—

(a) payments under a magistrates' court maintenance order;

(b) payment of sum to be paid under certain convictions;

(c) payment of a sum due under a legal aid contribution order (s. 1 (3), *ibid.*).

A county court may make an attachment of earnings order to secure—

(a) payments under a High Court or a county court maintenance order;

(b) payment of a judgment debt or balance of £5 or more (*Ord.* 25, *r.* 83(4));

(c) payments under a county court administration order (s. 1 (2), *ibid.*).

Maintenance orders to which the Act applies are set out in Sched. 1 to the 1971 Act, and include orders for periodical or other payments under the Matrimonial Causes Act, 1973, Part II, formerly the Matrimonial Proceedings and Property Act, 1970, Part I, and certain orders under the Guardianship of Minors Act, 1971.

The term "judgment debt" does not include a maintenance order or an administration order (s. 2 (c), *ibid.*).

The following may not, *inter alia*, be treated as earnings: (a) pay or allowances of a member of H.M. forces; and (b) wages of a seaman other than wages as a seaman in a fishing boat (s. 24 (2), *ibid.*).

Members of H.M. Forces

Deductions may be made from servicemen's pay under the various statutes, such as the Army Act, 1955, to satisfy judgment debts. Deductions are made at the discretion of the Defence Council or any officer authorised by them. Cases should not be referred to the Service authorities unless it has been established that the serviceman will not comply with the order voluntarily. The judgment creditor or his solicitor may then refer the case to the appropriate authority, forwarding a copy of the judgment or order giving particulars of the amount already paid and the amount owing.

The addresses of the Service authorities are as follows:

Navy
> Ministry of Defence,
> Naval Personnel (Pay) Division,
> Old Admiralty Building,
> Whitehall, London, S.W.1.

Army
> Officers—Ministry of Defence,
> PF 2d (Army),
> Lansdowne House,
> Berkeley Square,
> London W1X 6AA.

Other ranks—the appropriate regimental pay office (addresses published in the Army List).

R.A.F.
> Officers—Ministry of Defence,
> DPS 2 (RAF),
> Adastral House,
> Theobalds Road,
> London WC1X 8RU
> Other ranks—Ministry of Defence,
> DGPM (RAF),
> Eastern Avenue,
> Barnwood,
> Gloucester.

Index

Each county court keeps an index of debtors residing within its district against whom there are in force attachment of earnings orders, which have been made by that court, or notice of which has been received from another court. Any person, who has a judgment or order against another person believed to be residing within the district of the court, may cause a search to be made in the index (*Ord.* 25, *r.* 78).

Requirements for search:

  (a) Request for search (*Form* Ex. 218);

  (b) *Fee:* 25p (No. 22 (iv));

  (c) Stamped addressed envelope if search made by post.

Form Ex. 218 is supplied by the court and provides for a certificate as to the result of the search.

Application for attachment of earnings order

The application is made to the court for the district in which the debtor resides. If the debtor does not reside within England or Wales, or the creditor does not know where he resides, the application may be made to the court in which the judgment or order was obtained (*Ord.* 25, *r.* 79).

Where the creditor applies for attachment of earnings orders in respect of two or more debtors jointly liable, the application is made to the court for the district in which any of the debtors resides; but if the judgment or order was given or made by any such court, the application must be made to that court (*Ord.* 25, *r.* 79 (3)).

In the case of a maintenance order made in a county court, the application must be made to that county court (*Ord.* 25, *r.* 94 (2)). It would appear that in respect of divorce costs, the application must be made to the court where the debtor resides.

The persons who may apply are (s. 3(1) of the 1971 Act)—

  (a) the person to whom payment under the relevant adjudication is required to be made (whether directly or through an officer of any court);

  (b) in the case of an administration order, any one of the creditors scheduled to the order;

  (c) the debtor, where the application is to secure maintenance payments; the debtor may apply on the making of the maintenance order or on an order varying the maintenance order (*Ord.* 25, *r.* 94 (4)).

Where a creditor desires to make an application to a county court other than the county court in which the judgment or order was obtained, he must apply for the transfer of the proceedings to the appropriate court under *Ord.* 25, *rr.* 48 and 79 (4).

Requirements:
- (a) Letter applying for transfer and stating defendant's address;
- (b) *Fee:* 15p (No. 52).

The court sends a certificate of judgment or order to the named court and the registrar of that court gives the proceedings a fresh plaint number and sends notice of the transfer in *Form* 90A to both parties.

Requirements for issue of application for attachment of earnings order:
- (a) Application in *Form* 402 and copy for service;
- (b) Plaint note or originating process;
- (c) If service is to be by post, certificate in *Form* 6;
- (d) *Fee:* see below;

In addition, if judgment is of a court other than a county court:
- (e) Office copy of judgment or order;
- (f) Affidavit in *Form* 175;
- (g) Where a writ of *fi. fa.* issued, office copy of sheriff's return; or,

In addition, if to enforce a magistrates' court order:
- (e) Certified copy of order;
- (f) If payments are required to be made to the clerk of the magistrates' court, a certificate by him as to the matters mentioned in *Form* 175, otherwise, an affidavit in *Form* 175;

In addition, if against a partner in a firm:
- (aa) Affidavit in *Form* 174 and copy.

The name and address of the employer must be stated in the application.

The application issues for the balance of debt and costs in the case of a judgment debt (see *Form* 402) (s. 6 (4) of the 1971 Act). The balance may not include the costs of an execution not recovered thereunder (*Ord.* 25, *r.* 86 (2)).

An application under s. 32 of the Matrimonial Clauses Act, 1973, formerly s. 10 of the Matrimonial Proceedings and Property Act, 1970, for leave to enforce the payment of arrears which became due more than twelve months before the application, must be made in that application (*Ord.* 25, *r.* 94 (3)).

The debtor must be in default (s. 3 (3) of the 1971 Act). In the case of an attachment of earnings order in respect of a maintenance order, unless the debtor applies, fifteen days must have elapsed since the making of the maintenance order and the debtor's failure to make payment must be due to wilful refusal or culpable neglect (s. 3 (2) and (5), *ibid.*).

Fees (No. 22):

    (i) To secure maintenance payments, 50p.

    (ii) Other than on an application for a consolidated attachment order, to secure payment of a judgment debt:

        For a sum not over £10, £1

        Over £10 and up to £20, £2

        Over £20 and up to £30, £3

        Over £30 and up to £50, £4

        Over £50 and up to £100, £5

        Over £100, £6.

    In addition, if service by bailiff and not by post, 50p

The date of hearing is marked on the plaint note or other document or schedule produced by applicant.

Service.—The court prepares notice of hearing in *Form* 403 and copy. The copy of the application with notice of hearing in *Form* 403, a form of reply in *Form* 404 and a franked addressed envelope addressed to the court, are served on the debtor in the same manner as an ordinary summons. Service must be effected not less than twenty-one clear days before the return day. If service is to be effected by post, a certificate in *Form* 6 must be filed. If the application is not served, notice of non-service is sent to the judgment creditor. It is not clear whether the rules as to successive ordinary summonses apply.

Leave of the judge is required to serve an application on a debtor who resides out of England and Wales (*Ord.* 8, *r.* 42 (2)). Application for leave is made by affidavit under *Ord.* 8, *r.* 44.

Interlocutory matters.—Unless the debtor pays the balance owing, he must within fourteen days of service upon him, file in the court office a reply in *Form* 404 setting out particulars of his expenditure and income and the name and address of his employer, if any. The franked addressed envelope served with the notice of hearing is supplied for this purpose. The court sends a copy of the reply to the judgment creditor (*Ord.* 25, *r.* 81).

If the debtor does not file a reply, the court may order him to do so (s. 14 (1) of the 1971 Act). If the application has been served personally upon him, or the court is satisfied that it has come to his knowledge in sufficient time, he may be taken to have committed an offence under s. 23(2) (*c*) or (*f*) of the 1971 Act.

The court may send a notice to the employer requesting him to give the court a statement of the debtor's earnings (*Ord.* 25, *r.* 82). If the employer does not send a statement in compliance with the request, the court may compel him to do so (ss. 14 (1) (*b*) and 23 (2) (*c*), *ibid.*). An order to file the statement must be served personally (*Ord.* 25, *r.* 92). There is no settled practice as to the time when the court will on its own motion send a request to the employer, but probably before the first hearing when the name and address of the employer are known and after the time for filing a reply has expired. The request is in *Form* Ex. 220, which is not a pre-scribed form.

Hearing.—The hearing takes place before the registrar and in chambers. Evidence in support and in answer may be given by affidavit. If the creditor does not appear, he may file an affidavit or a request in writing for the court to proceed in his absence (*Ord.* 25, *r.* 83). Otherwise, the proceedings may be struck out under *Ord.* 23, *r.* 2.

If the debtor has not filed a reply, his attendance may be required. If he does not attend the hearing, an order may be made in *Form* 179 for him to attend at an adjourned hearing (*Ord.* 25, *rr.* 43 and 84). The order must be served on the debtor personally not less than five clear days before the day fixed for the adjourned hearing. The order is usually served by bailiff (no fee). No conduct money is payable. If the debtor does not attend, the judge may make an order for him to be imprisoned for not more than fourteen days (s. 23 (1) of the 1971 Act). The order is in *Form* 179A. The debtor may apply for the revocation of the order, or for his discharge, if in custody, and *Ord.* 25, *r.* 43 (4) to (7), applies.

If the debtor does not reply or attend, an order may also be made requiring him to file a reply in *Form* 404 if he has not already done so.

Practice varies as between courts. An attachment of earnings order will not normally be made until a reply in Form 404 has been received, from the debtor. The different courses open before and after hearing are as follows:

(a) *Attachment of earnings application served but not personally.*

   After fourteen days from service, no reply having been received the court may make an order for the production of a statement of earnings. The order is in *Form* Ex. 221 and orders the debtor to file a reply within a specified time, for example, four days. The official view is that the order should be served personally. It the debtor fails to obey the order, a notice to show cause in *Form* Ex. 233 may be issued for hearing before the judge. This notice must be served personally and the judge has power to commit.

This course has a possible disadvantage in that delay might occur because there are two processes requiring personal service.

(b) *Attachment of earnings application served personally.*

   If the debtor fails to file a reply within fourteen days of service, a notice to show cause in *Form* Ex. 233 may be issued without further order. See *Ord.* 25, *r.* 81(4) (proviso).

   Where a debtor fails to obey or otherwise to comply with the notice in *Form* Ex. 233, the order of commitment (or warrant) is in C.C.R. *Form* 279.

It is intended that these procedures should to be taken before the application comes before the registrar for hearing. However, the creditor is not fully aware of what is happening and is not sure whether the court acts of its own motion. If a return day is given within a month, there may be insufficient time to serve process personally.

The procedure that seems to be implied by the rules is that which used to be followed in judgment summonses. The date of hearing is fixed about one month from the date of issue, with the intent that a final order be made on the return day. If the debtor does not attend or file information in reply, the hearing is adjourned and the debtor is ordered to attend at the adjourned hearing. This procedure is known as the "Form 179 procedure". The order is in *Form* Ex. 231, which is *Form* 179 adapted, and is served personally. A supplementary order is sometimes made that the debtor file a reply in *Form* 404 within a specified time, for example, seven days. This order is served by post. If the debtor fails to file a reply, the order in *Form* 179 is issued for service. Notice of adjournment is given to the creditor, who is aware of the progress of the application.

Costs.—Where costs are allowed, they are the same as those which would be allowed on a judgment summons. The scale of costs is determined by the amount for which the application was issued (*Ord.* 25, *r.* 85). In the case of a maintenance order, the scale of costs is determined by the amount of the arrears due at the issue of the application (*Ord.* 25, *r.* 94 (5)). For the amount of solicitors' costs, see Appendix I, *infra.*

Form of order.—"Attachable earnings" are defined in Sched. 3 to the Act of 1971 and are briefly the amount of earnings paid to the debtor by his employer after deductions for income tax, national insurance and superannuation.

"Earnings" are defined in s. 24 of the Act, and include commission and overtime pay.

"Protected earnings rate" is defined in s. 6 (5) (*b*) and is the rate below which, having regard to the debtor's resources and needs, the court thinks it reasonable that the earnings actually paid to him should not be reduced. Protected earnings are normally calculated by reference to the rates of supplementary benefits under the National Insurance Acts together with the rent or mortgage payments. The rates as from the 1st October 1973 are as follows:

Requirements of persons other than blind persons—

		£
(a) married couple		11.65
(b) person living alone or householder not falling within sub-paragraph (a) of this paragraph who is directly responsible for household necessities and rent (if any)		7.15
(c) any other person aged—		
(i) not less than 18 years		5.70
(ii) less than 18 but not less than 16 years ...		4.40
(iii) less than 16 but not less than 13 years ...		3.70
(iv) less than 13 but not less than 11 years ...		3.00
(v) less than 11 but not less than 5 years ...		2.45
(vi) less than 5 years		2.05

The principle is confirmed in *Billington v. Billington* (1973), *The Times*, 13th November.

"Normal deduction rate" is defined in s. 6 (5) (a) and is the rate at which the court thinks it reasonable for the debtor's earnings to be applied to meeting his liability.

The form of order for a judgment debt is in *Form* 405, and for maintenance, in *Form* 407, and informs the employer of the protected earnings rate and the normal deduction rate.

An order may be made attaching a debtor's earnings but suspended while he makes regular payments as may be ordered. The order is in *Form* Ex. 234 and is made where a debtor's employment might be jeopardised if his employer became aware of the order attaching earnings. If the debtor makes default, the creditor may send a request by letter to the registrar to issue the order.

An attachment of earnings order is sent by post to the debtor and to the employer. If the order is to enforce a judgment or order of the High Court or a magistrates' court, a copy of the order is sent to the proper officer of those courts (*Ord.* 25, *r.* 86). A booklet is sent with the order to the employer to explain how the deductions should be made. The copy of the order to the debtor informs him that he must inform the court of any change in employment.

Deductions by the employer from the debtor's earnings are made in accordance with Sched. 3 to the 1971 Act. Priority as between orders is set out in this schedule. In the case of *judgment* debts and payments under an *administration order*, the employer deducts no more than the amount of the normal deduction rate; he does not deduct for arrears from previous days. In the case of other deductions, which include maintenance and amounts due under a conviction, the employer deducts first any arrears which have accrued from previous pay days when the attachable earnings fell short of the protected earnings rate. Priority is determined by the respective dates on which the orders were made, but the employer must give priority to orders which are not to secure judgment debts or administration orders; for instance, maintenance deductions would have priority.

The employer is allowed on each deduction to deduct from the debtor's earnings, in addition, 5p towards his administrative costs (s. 7 (4), *ibid.*).

The employer is under no liability for non-compliance with the order until seven days have elapsed since the service (s. 7 (1), *ibid.*). If he does not have the debtor in his employment or the debtor ceases to be in his employment, he must give notice of the fact to the court within ten days of service of the order or cesser (s. 7 (2), *ibid.*). If an employer ceases to have the debtor in his employment the order lapses but the court may direct it to another employer (s. 9(4)). There appears to be no provision that the court should notify the judgment creditor if a debtor leaves his employment.

The employer pays the sums deducted from the debtor's earnings to the court and the sums in court are paid out under the normal procedure.

There are no rules which prescribe that the court should

notify a creditor when an employer makes no payment into court. The court does not act on its own initiative to enquire from the employer any reason for payments not being received. In such cases, the creditor should write to the court requiring an enquiry to be made and to request the court to take action where an employer refuses or neglects to give the information required.

Consolidated attachment order

Such an order is made to secure the payment of any number of *judgment* debts. (s. 17 of the 1971 Act).

Order 25, *r*. 90, applies. No forms are prescribed by rule but *Form* Ex. 235 is used by courts for a consolidated attachment order.

A county court may make a consolidated attachment order—

(*a*) where two or more attachment of earnings orders are in force to secure the payment of *judgment* debts by the same debtor, or

(*b*) where, on an application for an attachment or earnings order to secure a *judgment* debt or for a consolidated attachment order, it appears to the court that an attachment of earnings order is already in force.

A consolidated attachment order in respect of maintenance orders may be made only in a magistrates' court (s. 17 (1), *ibid*.) and not in a county court (*Ord*. 25, *r*. 94 (11)).

A consolidated attachment order may be made—

(*a*) on an application by a judgment debtor; or

(*b*) on an application by a judgment creditor who has obtained or is entitled to apply for an attachment of earnings order (*Ord*. 25, *r*. 90 (2)); or

(*c*) on the request of an employer (*Ord*. 25, *r*. 90(5)); or

(*d*) by the court of its own motion (*Ord*. 25, *r*. 90 (6)).

A *judgment debtor* may apply—

(*a*) in the proceedings in which any attachment of earnings order is in force; or

(*b*) at the hearing of an application for an attachment of earnings order.

The debtor applies in accordance with *Ord.* 13, *r.* 1.
Requirements:
> Application in *Form* Ex. 23 and copies for service.

Copies of the application are served by post on the judgment creditor in the proceedings and also on any other judgment creditor who has obtained an attachment of earnings order, which is in force, giving one clear day's notice (*Ord.* 25, *r.* 90 (3)). *Fee,* No. 22 (iii), is deducted from payments into court.

A *judgment creditor's* application must—

(a) if the judgment which he seeks to enforce was given "by the court to which the application is made", be made in accordance with *Ord.* 13, *r.* 1, in the proceedings in which the judgment was obtained (and *Ord.* 25, *rr.* 80 and 81, do not apply);

(b) in any other case, be made by originating application (and *Ord.* 25, *rr.* 80 (1) and (2) and 81, do not apply) (*Ord.* 25, *r.* 90 (4)).

A consolidated attachment order is also an attachment of earnings order (s. 17 (2) of the 1971 Act). *Order* 25, *r.* 79, applies. Therefore, an application by a judgment creditor for a consolidated attachment order must be made in the court for the district in which the debtor resides, except where the debtor does not reside in England or Wales or there are joint debtors, and then *Ord.* 25, *r.* 79 (2) and (3), applies.

If the application is made under *Ord.* 13, *r.* 1, it may be made in *Form* Ex. 23 with copies for service. Copies are served by post on the judgment debtor and every person, who, to the knowledge of the applicant, has obtained an attachment of earnings order which is in force to secure a *judgment debt.*

If the application is to be made by originating application, requirements:

(a) Originating application in *Form* 23 with copies for service;

(b) If service is to be by post, certificate in *Form* 6;
> In addition, if judgment is of a court other than a county court:

(c) Office copy of judgment or order;

(*d*) Affidavit in *Form* 175;

(*e*) Where writ of *fi.fa.* issued, office copy of sheriff's return;

(*f*) *Fee:* if service by bailiff, 50p; otherwise Fee No. 22 (iii) is deducted from payments into court.

The judgment debtor and every person who, to the knowledge of the applicant, has obtained an attachment of earnings order which is in force to secure a *judgment debt*, is made a respondent (*Ord.* 25, *r.* 90 (4)).

Rules as to originating applications then apply.

It would seem that a county court judgment should be transferred to the appropriate court under *Ord.* 25, *rr.* 48 and 79 (4), before an application is made and then that it should be made under *Ord.* 13, *r.* 1.

Regarding an *employer*, a person to whom two or more attachment of earnings orders are directed to secure the payment of *judgment* debts by the same debtor, may request the courts in writing to make a consolidated attachment order. No form is prescribed for the request. On receipt of such a request, the court must fix a hearing at which the request will be considered and give notice thereof to the debtor and the judgment creditors. No form of notice is prescribed (*Ord.* 25, *r.* 90 (5)).

Regarding the *court acting of its own motion*, where an application is made for an attachment of earnings order and there is another order already in force, the court may make a consolidated attachment order after giving all persons concerned an opportunity of being heard. No form of notice of hearing is prescribed (*Ord.* 25, *r.* 90 (6)).

As to *any judgment creditor*, where a consolidated attachment order is already in force, any creditor to whom another judgment debt is owed, may apply to the court, by which the order is made, for the consolidated attachment order to be extended to secure the payment of his judgment debt. Such an application is to be treated as an application for a consolidated attachment order (*Ord.* 25, *r.* 90 (7)). It would appear that the debtor need not be in arrear for the creditor to be in a position to apply. If the consolidated order was made in the same court, the creditor may apply under *Ord.* 13, *r.* 1, in his own action. Otherwise, he must apply by originating application under *Ord.* 25, *r.* 90 (4).

Payment into court.—Where money is received by the court under a consolidated attachment order, the fee is first deducted. *Fee:* for every £1 paid into court or part thereof in respect of debts due, 5p (No. 22 (iii)). The remainder is distributed by way of dividends declared from time to time (*Ord.* 25, *r.* 90 (8)).

Transfer of attachment order

Where the court, which has under consideration the making of a consolidated attachment order, is not the court which has made the other attachment of earnings order, the registrar may request the registrar of the other court to transfer the matter to his court (*Ord.* 25, *r.* 91 (1)).

An attachment of earnings order may be transferred to another county court if the matter could more conveniently proceed there whether because the debtor has moved his residence or otherwise (*Ord.* 25, *r.* 91 (2)).

Cesser and discharge and variation

In the case of a judgment debt, where the whole amount has been paid, the court gives notice to the employer that no further compliance with the order is required (s. 12 (2) of the 1971 Act). On the penultimate payment being received from the employer, the court sends him notice in *Form* Ex. 223 informing him of the sum on payment of which the order will be satisfied.

In the case of a maintenance order, when the total payments exceed the aggregate or arrears and current payments under the maintenance order and the normal deduction rate exceeds the rate of payments required by the maintenance order, and no proceedings for the variation or discharge of the attachment of earnings order are pending, the registrar sends a notice in *Form* 409 to the employer and to the debtor (s. 10 (1) and (2), *ibid.*). The notice informs the debtor that unless he applies to the court within fourteen days after the date of the notice for an order discharging the attachment of earnings order or varying it, the court will make an order varying the attachment of earnings order by reducing the normal deduction rate to the rate of payments required by the maintenance order or a lower rate (*Ord.* 25, *r.* 94 (9)). The debtor applies on *Form* Ex. 23 under *Ord.* 13, *r.* 1. It should be noted that a "lump sum" in matrimonial proceedings is within the term "maintenance order".

When an attachment of earnings order ceases to have effect on the making of an order of commitment or the issue of a warrant of commitment for the enforcement of the debt, the court gives notice of the cesser to the employer (*Ord.* 25, *r.* 88). No form is prescribed.

The court may make an order discharging or varying an attachment of earnings order (s. 9 (1) of the 1971 Act). A party would apply for such an order on notice in *Form* Ex. 23.

An attachment of earnings order may be discharged, or varied—

(a) where it appears that the employer or person to whom the order is directed does not have the debtor in his employment (*Ord.* 25, *r.* 89 (2)), but the court may vary and direct the order to another employer (*ibid.*, *r.* 89 (3));

(b) where the court makes or is notified of another order which is not to secure a judgment debt or payments under an administration order (*Ord.* 25, *r.* 89 (4));

(c) where an administration order is made or an order for the debtor to produce a list of his creditors with a view to the making of an administration order (*Ord.* 25, *r.* 89 (5));

(d) on the making of a consolidated attachment of earnings order—the court may discharge an earlier order (*Ord.* 25, *r.* 89 (6));

(e) on the making of a receiving order or an order of adjudication (*Ord.* 25, *r.* 89 (7));

(*f*) where the court grants leave to issue execution (*Ord.* 25, *r.* 89 (8));

(*g*) on application by the debtor or creditor where there is a change in the debtor's means (*Ord.* 24, *rr.* 18 and 19).

The court may make an order discharging or varying an attachment of earnings order of its own motion in the above circumstances, but must give notice to the debtor and judgment creditor of the time and place at which the question will be considered, unless the court thinks it unnecessary in the circumstances to do so (*Ord.* 25, *r.* 89 (1) and (9)). No form of notice is prescribed.

Other matters

High Court maintenance order.—Where an attachment of earnings order made by the High Court designates the registrar of a county court as the collecting officer, the registrar sends notice in *Form* 408 to the employer (*Ord.* 25, *r.* 94 (7)). *Order* 25, *r.* 94 (8), applies as to cessation and variation.

Enforcement.—Orders are enforced under the penal and disciplinary provisions of *Ord.* 34 as applied by *Ord.* 25, *rr.* 92 and 93 except where the *Form* 179 procedure applies.

Application to determine whether particular payments are earnings.—Such an application is made in writing to the registrar. He thereupon fixes a date and time for hearing and gives notice to the employer, debtor, the judgment creditor, and, where applicable, the collecting officer of the magistrates' court (s. 16, *ibid.*, and *Ord.* 25, *r.* 87). No forms are prescribed.

CHARGING ORDERS

Charging orders may be made under the Partnership Act, 1890, s. 23. *Order* 25, *rr.* 4 or 5, apply, and *Ord.* 30 applies as to the appointment of a receiver. See procedure in High

Court, in notes to R.S.C., *Ord.* 81, *r.* 10, in *Supreme Court Practice.*

Charging orders may be made under the Solicitors Act, 1957, s. 72, in an action in the court upon property recovered or preserved through the instrumentality of the solicitor. *Order* 46, *r.* 2 (2), applies.

The above charging orders are rare.

Charging orders on land

A county court may, for the purpose of enforcing a judgment or order *thereof* for the payment of money to a person, by order impose on any such land or interest in land of the debtor as may be specified in the order a charge for securing the payment of any moneys due or to become due under the judgment or order (s. 141 (1) of the Act). A judgment or order, etc., of any court which is enforceable as if it were a county court judgment or order may be similarly enforced (s. 141 (4)). Note *Ord.* 25, *r.* 7A.

A charging order may not be made effectively upon the interest of one of joint owners of land, since a joint tenancy is held on a trust for sale and the debtor's interest would be in the proceeds of sale, which are not land (*Irani Finance, Ltd.* v. *Singh and Others* [1970] 3 All E.R. 199). A charging order may be made against two defendants owning land jointly (*National Westminster Bank* v. *Allen* [1971] 3 All E.R. 201).

Order 25, *r.* 7, applies.

Requirements:

(*a*) Application in *Form* Ex. 23 setting out the facts and copy for service;

(*b*) Plaint note or originating process;

(*c*) *Fee* (No. 46): 50p.

An application for a charging order may be joined with an application to appoint a receiver to entitle the judgment creditor to the benefit of the charging order as against a trustee in bankruptcy.

The general rules as to applications (*Ord.* 13, *r.* 1) apply. Service may be by ordinary post. The application must be made to a judge. The order is in *Form* 366.

An application to discharge a charging order may be made in the same proceedings by application in *Form* Ex. 23. The order should provide for vacating the registration of the charge. There is no rule specifically applying to the procedure.

A charging order is enforceable as if it were an equitable charge created by the debtor by writing under his hand (s. 141 (3)). It seems that originating proceedings must be commenced to enforce the charge. They must be commenced in the court in which the order was made (*Ord.* 2, *r.* 2), presumably by action under s. 52 (1) (*c*). The summons would be in *Form* 20. The limit of the county court equity jurisdiction is disregarded (s. 141 (3)).

For forms of order, see editorial forms in the *County Court Practice:* order for sale following charging order on land, Form (U), and order of registrar following order for sale of land under charging order, Form (V).

Charging orders on securities

Order 25, *r.* 6A, applies to applications for an order to impose a charge on the beneficial interest of a judgment debtor in—

(*a*) any United Kingdom government stock, funds or annuities, and stock, shares, debentures or debenture stock of any company registered under any general Act of Parliament, and

(*b*) any dividend of or interest payable on such stock.

The charge must be for the purpose of securing payment of an ascertained sum of money due or to become due under a judgment or order of the court. The order has the same effect as, and is enforced as if it were, a valid charge effectively made by the judgment debtor.

Requirements:

(*a*) Application in *Form* Ex. 23 setting out the facts and copy for service;

(*b*) Plaint note or originating process.

There appears to be no fee prescribed.

The application is made to a judge, or with leave of the judge, to a registrar. The general rule (*Ord.* 13, *r.* 1) as to applications applies.

The order is in *Form* 366. The order is served on the judgment debtor and on the Bank of England or the company concerned, as the case may be.

Proceedings to enforce the charge may not be taken until six months from the date of the order, and must be commenced in the court in which the order was made (*Ord.* 2, *r.* 2A). On the application of the judgment debtor or any other person interested in the securities, the order may at any time be discharged or varied, on terms as to costs, by the judge or registrar (cf. R.S.C., *Ord.* 50, *r.* 7).

RECEIVERS (*Ord.* 30)

A general power is given to county courts to appoint a receiver by s. 74 of the Act. The power to appoint a receiver by way of equitable execution in relation to all legal estates and interests in land is given in s. 142 of the Act. The judge may appoint a receiver of his own motion or on application. The order is in *Form* 242, 243, 244, or, in the case of equitable execution, 245. The recital in the forms of order implies that an affidavit in support of an application is required.

The procedure is set out in *Ord.* 30.

Equitable execution.—An application to appoint a receiver by way of equitable execution is made to the judge on notice. Requirements:

    (a) Application in *Form* Ex. 23 and copy for service;
    (b) Affidavit in support and copy for service;
    (c) Plaint note and originating process;
    (d) *Fee* (No. 44): for every £2 or part thereof due under the judgment or order, 5p; maximum £2.

The judge, in determining whether it is expedient to make an order, must have regard to the amount of debt and costs, the amount which would probably be obtained by the receiver and the probable cost of his appointment (*Ord.* 30, *r.* 11). The requisite costs and security are set out in *Ord.* 30, *r.* 12.

An order is most commonly made to receive rents. The order is in *Form* 245.

INFERIOR COURTS JUDGMENTS EXTENSION
ACT, 1882 (*Ord.* 42)

Order 42 sets out the procedure for extending judgments of inferior courts from Scotland and Northern Ireland to inferior courts in England and Wales, and *vice versa*. The *County Court Practice* sets out the relevant sections of the Act in notes under *Ord.* 42.

A certificate under this Act of 1882 is not granted until after the time for appealing has elapsed (s. 3) and may not be registered more than twelve months after the date of judgment (s. 4). If twelve months have expired, then a fresh action can be brought on the judgment.

An application for the grant of a certificate is made by letter. An affidavit is not usually required. The certificate is in *Form* 347 and is issued with a copy.

Fee: 25p (No. 28 (i)).

The fee and solicitor's costs of 25p (if affidavit, 35p) are added to the certificate.

When a certificate is received for registration, the address of the defendant being within the district, the court seals the copy certificate and returns it to the judgment creditor (*Ord.* 42, *r.* 9).

Fee: 5p (No. 28 (ii)).

This fee and further solicitor's costs of 25p for registration are added to the balance due.

The usual *præcipe* for the further process is filed and the usual fee paid. A warrant of execution is in *Form* 348, and judgment summons in *Form* 348A.

An attachment of earnings order may be made (Attachment of Earnings Act, 1971, ss. 1 (2) and 2 (c)).

GARNISHEE PROCEEDINGS
(*Ord.* 27)

Proceedings for attachment of debts are known as garnishee proceedings.

A person who has obtained a judgment or order for the payments of money may take proceedings to obtain payment to him of the amount of any debt owing or accruing to the judgment debtor from any other person (called "the garnishee") or so much thereof as may be sufficient to satisfy the judgment or order and the costs of the garnishee proceedings (*Ord*. 27, *r*. 1).

As to what debts are attachable and what not attachable, see notes after *Ord*. 27, *r*. 1, in the *County Court Practice* for 1973, on p. 562 *et seq*., and in the *Supreme Court Practice*, in notes after R.S.C., *Ord*. 49, *r*. 1. As to debts not yet payable, see note to *Ord*. 27, *r*. 3, in *County Court Practice* for 1973, on p. 565.

As to attaching *deposit accounts* in banks, s. 143 of the Act and *Ord*. 27, *r*. 1A, apply.

Where there is *money in court* due to a judgment debtor, the judgment creditor may not take garnishee proceedings in respect thereof, but may apply to the judge on notice for an order that the money or so much thereof as may be necessary to satisfy the judgment debt and costs may be paid to the judgment creditor. On the filing of the notice of application the registrar must retain the money in court until the application has been heard (*Ord*. 27, *r*. 18). The application can be made in *Form* Ex. 23. *Fee:* 5p for every £2 or part thereof of the money in court (or so much thereof as will satisfy the applicant's debt and costs); maximum £2 (No. 54 (ii)).

Garnishee proceedings may be taken notwithstanding that the debt owing or accruing from the garnishee exceeds £750 (*Ord*. 27, *r*. 2).

Venue.—Garnishee proceedings may be taken in the court where the judgment debtor could have sued the garnishee under *Ord*. 2, *r*. 1, that is, generally where the debtor might issue an ordinary summons in respect of the debt (*Ord*. 27, *r*. 3).

Requirements:
    (*a*) Affidavit in *Form* 205 (supplied by the court) by judgment creditor or his solicitor;

(b) If not commenced in the court where judgment or order obtained, certificate of judgment;

(c) Plaint note or originating process;

(d) *Fees:* 5p for every £1 or part; maximum £5 (No. 54(i)); if service by bailiff and garnishee is not a limited company, 50p (No. 4 (i));

(e) Stamped addressed envelope, if by post.

It is convenient to file also an ordinary summons *præcipe* as a concise statement of the parties.

The garnishee summons is allotted a plaint number and a plaint note is usually issued for the purpose of giving the judgment creditor notice of date and time of hearing.

Solicitor's costs entered on garnishee summons are as follows:—

For sum exceeding £5 and up to £20—

Service by court	£1.50
Service by solicitor	£2.00

Exceeding £20 and up to £100—

Service by court	£3.00
Service by solicitor	£4.00

Exceeding £100—

Service by court	£6.00
Service by solicitor	£7.00

The summons in *Form* 206 is prepared by the court. It must be served personally on the garnishee not less than fourteen clear days before the return day. When served on the garnishee, it binds in his hands so much of the debts owing or accruing from him to the judgment debtor as will satisfy the debt due and the costs entered on the summons (*Ord.* 27, *r.* 5). If the garnishee is a bank, the summons must be served at the registered office, which is usually in London, even though the account to be garnisheed is at a branch. It is then the practice to serve a copy of the summons also at the branch office.

When the garnishee has been served, the registrar must serve a copy of the summons on the judgment debtor with a notice in *Form* 207, not less than six clear days before the return day. This may be served by post (*Ord.* 27, *r.* 6).

Payment into court is provided for in *Ord.* 27, *r.* 7. Notice of payment into court is sent by the court to the judgment creditor in *Form* 208 or 209, and to the judgment debtor in *Form* 210. If the judgment was obtained in another court, notice is sent to that court (*Ord.* 27, *r.* 12); no form is prescribed.

Where money is paid into court by the garnishee and accepted by the judgment creditor, the registrar may on production of the consent in writing of the judgment debtor order the money to be paid out before the return day, or, in the absence of the judgment debtor, the registrar may on the return day make such order (including an order as to costs) as may be just (*Ord.* 27, *rr.* 8 and 20).

Order 27, *rr.* 9 to 11 and 16, provide for the procedure on the hearing.

Any costs allowed to the judgment creditor which are not ordered to be paid by the garnishee personally, shall, unless otherwise ordered, be retained by the judgment creditor out of the money recovered by him in the garnishee proceedings in priority to the amount due under the judgment or order (*Ord.* 27, *r.* 14). Costs of hearing are provided for in Item 8 in the Higher Scales of Costs. Part III of App. D applies in the Lower Scale. Costs may be allowed in respect of amounts exceeding £5, even though they do not exceed £75 (*Ord.* 47, *r.* 5 (4)(*b*)(ii)).

Where garnishee proceedings are taken in a court other than the court in which the judgment or order was obtained, a copy of the order is sent to the other court and notice of any payment into court (*Ord.* 27, *r.* 12).

It should be remembered that, if a receiving order is made against the defendant before the money has been paid out of court, the trustee in bankruptcy can claim it (*George* v. *Thompson's Trustee* [1949] 1 All E.R. 554). He may also claim it where the money is not paid out before notice of the presentation of any bankruptcy petition by or against the debtor, or of the commission of any available act of bankruptcy (Bankruptcy Act, 1914, s. 40).

INTERPLEADER PROCEEDINGS OTHER THAN UNDER EXECUTION

Order 28, *rr.* 16 to 22, applies. The application is made in the court where the applicant is sued, or, if he has not been sued, to the court in which he might have been sued.

Notes in the *Supreme Court Practice* after R.S.C., *Ord.* 17, *r.* 1, set out the cases when interpleader proceedings are appropriate.

Fees: no fee if applicant is a defendant; otherwise, as for plaint fee for a sum of money calculated on the amount or value of the money or goods the subject matter of the proceedings (No. 59); for service by bailiff, 50p each for place of service, unless service is on a limited company (No. 4).

PROCEEDINGS BY AND AGAINST EXECUTORS AND ADMINISTRATORS

Order 32 provides for the various forms of judgment and order against personal representatives. A warrant of execution against the goods of a deceased person is in *Form* 261.

PAYMENT INTO COURT BY TRUSTEES
(*Ord.* 38)

Where a person wishes to pay money or securities into court under the Trustee Act, 1925, s. 63, or to pay a debt or other thing in action into court under the Law of Property Act, 1925, s. 136, he must file an affidavit in *Form* 321 containing the information required thereby, and must pay the money or securities into court in accordance with the *County Court Funds Rules,* 1965, or lodge the thing in action in the court office. The costs incurred in the payment into court may be taxed and the amount of the taxed costs retained by the person making the payment (*Ord.* 38, *r.* 1).

The affidavit is first lodged for the registrar to give a direction that the money or security may be accepted. If he gives such a direction, the bill of costs is then lodged and an appointment given for taxation, the usual fees for taxation being paid. The bill of costs should not include the court fee for payment into court in the case of money, as this fee is deducted from the sum paid in. The money is invested in accordance with *County Court Funds Rules*, 1965.

The proceedings are under equity jurisdiction. The county court has jurisdiction, in the case of the Trustee Act, 1925, where the money or securities to be paid into court do not exceed in amount or value £5,000 and, in the case of the Law of Property Act, 1925, s. 136, where the amount or value of the debt or thing in action does not exceed £750 (Sched. I to the County Courts Act).

Fees: on payment into court, £1 plus 5p for every £4 or part thereof calculated on the amount of the money or value of the securities paid into court (No. 60) (where money is paid into court, this fee is deducted from the money); on taxation of the costs, where amount allowed does not exceed £5, 25p; where it exceeds £5 but not £100, for every £1 or part thereof allowed, 5p; where it exceeds £100, then £5 for the first £100 plus 5p for every £2 or part thereof over £100 (No. 19 (i)).

The power of paying trust money into court should only be exercised when it is difficult for trustees to obtain a discharge otherwise. Building societies sometimes pay money into court under the Trustee Act, 1925, s. 63, when they have become constructive trustees of surplus money arising out of the sale of a security and the mortgagor cannot be found.

Notice in *Form* 322 is sent to any person interested in the money or securities paid into court. Any application, such as for payment out, may be made to the judge *ex parte* (see *Ord.* 38, *r.* 2).

NEW TRIAL AND SETTING JUDGMENT ASIDE
(*Ord.* 37)

Both parties at trial (Ord. 37, r. 1)

The judge has power to order a new trial. An application may be made for a new trial on the day of the trial if both

parties are present, or at the first court held next after the
expiration of twelve days from the day of trial, or by leave
of the judge at any subsequent court. If not made on the
day of trial, the application may be in *Form* Ex. 23. It must
state the ground of the application and not less than six
clear days' notice must be given to the opposite party. The
registrar must, unless otherwise ordered, retain any money
in court until the application has been heard. No fee.

An order for a new trial is in *Form* 320 and is sent by the
court to both parties.

The principles upon which a new trial is granted are set
out in notes to *Ord.* 37, *r.* 1, in the *County Court Practice*,
1973, p. 600.

Judgment given in absence of defendant (Ord. 37, r. 2)

Where a defendant to an action or matter or a defendant
to a counterclaim does not appear at the hearing and a
judgment or order is given or made against him in his absence,
he may apply to have the judgment or order and any executions thereon set aside and for a new trial to be granted.
The application may, if the parties are present, be made on
the day on which the judgment or order was given or made
and, in any other case, must be made on notice. The applications must be made to the judge, if the judgment or order
was given or made by the judge, and, in any other case, to
the registrar.

The application may be made in *Form* Ex. 23. No fee.

Judgment in default (Ord. 37, r. 3)

Where, in a default action, judgment is entered in default
and the defendant satisfactorily explains his default and
satisfies the court that *he has a defence or counterclaim* which
ought to be heard, the court may set aside judgment and
execution thereon. The application may be made in *Form*
Ex. 23 and must be made on notice to the plaintiff. The
court may stay execution pending the hearing. If a stay is
required urgently, the application is placed before the registrar
personally, who normally grants the stay *ex parte*. No fee.

Where the defendant has no defence, then, if he is unable to come to an arrangement with the plaintiff as to payment, he can make an application for time to pay.

Irregularity (Ord. 37, r. 4)

The court may set aside proceedings for irregularity. The application must be made on notice and must state the objections to be relied upon. Such an application may not be granted unless made within a reasonable time, nor if the party applying has taken any step in the proceedings after knowledge of the irregularity. The application may be in *Form* Ex. 23 stating the objections relied on. No fee.

Failure of postal service (Ord. 37, r. 6)

Where a summons or other originating process has been served by post (under *Ord.* 8, *rr.* 8 or 14) and after judgment has been given or entered it appears to the court that the process did not come to the knowledge of the defendant in time, the court may *of its own motion* set aside the judgment and may give any direction or make any such order as the court may think just. Where a judgment has been so set aside, the court gives notice to the plaintiff.

APPEAL

From Registrar

Interlocutory applications (Ord. 13, r. 1 (h))

Where the registrar has made an order to which *Ord.* 13, *r.* 1, applies (the general rule on applications), any party who is dissatisfied may apply to the judge to vary or rescind the order. Application is in *Form* Ex. 23. No fee.

Taxation of costs

Objections to taxation of costs must be made within two days. *Order.* 47, *r.* 42, applies. See, *infra*.

Judgment or final order (Ord. 37, r. 5)

Any party affected by a judgment or final order of a registrar may, except where he has consented to the terms thereof, appeal to the judge. The appeal must be made on notice stating the grounds and the notice must be served within six days of the judgment or order appealed from. Execution may be stayed pending the hearing. Application is in *Form* Ex. 23. No fee.

From Judge

The provisions as to appeal from the judge or jury are contained in ss. 107 to 114 of the Act. Appeals are, usually, to the Court of Appeal.

An appeal lies to the Court of Appeal from the judge *in point of law* or *upon the admission or rejection of any evidence,* but no appeal is allowed, without leave of the judge, in an action founded on contract or tort where the debt or damage claimed does not exceed £20 (not being an action for recovery of land, or where the title to any hereditament has come into question, or where the relief sought includes an injunction); nor in an action of replevin where the amount of rent, or damage or value of the goods seized does not exceed £20; nor in interpleader proceedings where the money claimed, or the value of the goods claimed, does not exceed £20 (s. 108 of the Act).

An appeal lies to the Court of Appeal from a judge or jury on *any question of fact* in the following cases (s. 109 of the Act):—

    (*a*) any action founded on contract or tort or from money recoverable by statute, where either—

        (i) the debt, demand or damage claimed exceeds £200; or

        (ii) the relief sought includes an injunction; or

        (iii) the title to a hereditament comes in question and the net annual value for rating of the hereditament (or, in the case of an easement or licence, that of the hereditament in respect of which the easement or licence is claimed, or, on, through, over or under which it is claimed) exceeds £500;

    (*b*) an action for the recovery of land of a net annual value for rating exceeding £500;

(c) any action where there is a counterclaim to which either of the foregoing paragraphs would apply if the counterclaim had been the subject of a separate action;

(d) any matter transferred from the High Court under the Act relating to applications to attach debts, or levy an execution against a member of a firm for a partnership debt, where the debt in question exceeds £200;

(e) any proceedings in interpleader, or relating to any debt or things in action paid into court under the Law of Property Act, 1925, s. 136, where the amount or value exceeds £200

(f) any probate proceedings where the value of the estate (as stated in the affidavit) exceeds £500;

(g) any proceedings on an application under the Matrimonial Proceedings (Magistrates' Court) Act, 1960, s. 13A, and the Matrimonial Causes Act, 1973, ss. 3, 36 and 38, formerly the Matrimonial Proceedings and Property Act, 1970, ss. 11, 15 and 22.

Under (a), (b) or (c) above, an appeal may be brought in respect of any claim or counterclaim, notwithstanding that there could be no such appeal if that claim or counterclaim had been the subject of a separate action.

There is no appeal on a question of fact in proceedings in which either party is claiming possession of any premises if, by virtue of the Rent Act, 1968, s. 10, as it applies to Cases 1 to 8 in Sched. 3, or the Landlord and Tenant Act, 1954, s. 13 (4), the court can only grant possession on being satisfied that it is reasonable so to do.

There is no appeal as to an instalment order (*Capewell and Mason, Ltd.* v. *Kujore* [1968], 112 Sol. J. 824).

An appeal from an order made under the Guardianship of Minors Act, 1971, s. 16 (2), is to a Divisional Court of the Family Division of the High Court. R.S.C., *Ord.* 90, *r.* 9, applies. The time is twenty-eight days.

If an application for custody coincides with an application for an adoption order, the applications should be heard together. If appeals are brought against both orders, the appeal to the Family Division should be dismissed without giving reasons, so that both appeals may be heard together in the Court of Appeal since an appeal from an order made in an adoption application lies to the Court of Appeal (*Re E. (P.), an infant* [1969] 1 All E.R. 323).

An appeal from an order made under the Land Registration Act, 1925, is to a Divisional Court of the Chancery Division. R.S.C., *Ord.* 93, *r.* 10 (1), applies. The time is twenty-eight days.

Procedure.—Appeals to the Court of Appeal are made in accordance with the Rules of the Supreme Court. R.S.C., *Ord.* 59, applies. The appeal must be served within fourteen days, if it is an interlocutory order; twenty-one days if it is an order in bankruptcy or winding up; and, in every other case, six weeks. All periods count from the date of the judgment or order (R.S.C., *Ord.* 59, *rr.* 4 and 19). Notice of the appeal must be served on the registrar as well as on the parties.

A copy of the judge's note and a certificate of judgment (*Form* 141 (1)) are required. Application for them is made by letter setting out the purpose for which they are required. *Fees:* copy of judge's note, 20p per typewritten page if of A4, foolscap or smaller size (30p per page if larger) plus half these fees if a carbon copy is taken in addition (No. 66); for a photographic copy the fee per sheet is 10p if of A4, foolscap or smaller size or 20p if larger (No. 65); certificate of judgment, 5p (No. 68).

CERTIORARI, PROHIBITION AND MANDAMUS
(ss. 115 to 119 of the Act)

The High Court may, by order of certiorari or otherwise, order the removal into the High Court of any county court proceedings, if the High Court thinks it desirable that the proceedings should be heard and determined in the High Court (s. 115 (1) of the Act).

Application may be made to the High Court for an order of prohibition addressed to a county court (s. 116 (1) of the Act).

Any party requiring any act to be done by a judge or officer of a county court relating to the duties of his office may apply to the High Court for an order of mandamus (s. 118 of the Act).

Order 16, *r.* 20, applies in the case of certiorari and prohibition.

R.S.C., *Ord.* 53, applies to the proceedings in the High Court.

ADMIRALTY

Those courts having Admiralty jurisdiction are shown in a list at the end of the *County Court Practice* as prescribed by S.I. 1971 No. 1152.

Order 35 applies to Admiralty proceedings; *Ord.* 46, *r.* 15 to proceedings under the Merchant Shipping Act, 1894, s. 556; and *Ord.* 46, *r.* 6, to appeals under the Pilotage Act, 1913, s. 28.

There are two types of action in Admiralty, *in personam* and *in rem*. In an action *in rem*, a party proceeds against an owner of a ship or cargo without naming him.

Order 35, *r.* 2, applies as to venue.

Requirements on issue:

(*a*) Request or *præcipe* in *Form* 281;

(*b*) Particulars of claim and copy or copies for service;

(*c*) Plaint fee as for an ordinary summons.

Plaint note is issued. No date for hearing is fixed on issue

Form of summons is in *Form* 282 (*in rem*) or *Form* 283 (*in personam*). A solicitor accepting service of a summons *in rem* should sign a memorandum in *Form* 284 (not supplied by court).

As to entering an appearance, *Ord.* 35, *r*, 14, applies.

Requirements:

Request or *præcipe* in *Form* 286 with copies for sealing and service.

The defendant serves a sealed copy *Form* 286 on the plaintiff with notice in *Form* 287. These forms are not supplied by the court.

Section 83 of the Act and *Ord.* 35, *r.* 9, apply to the issue of a warrant of arrest of a vessel, aircraft or property.

Requirements:

(*a*) Affidavit containing particulars required by *Ord.* 35, *r.* 9;

(*b*) *Fee:* £2 (No. 12).

The warrant is issued in duplicate in *Form* 285.

The court notifies the local officer of Customs, by telephone or telegram if necessary, of the issue of the warrant so that the ship may be refused clearance. The bailiff completes the arrest. The plaintiffs and any other interested party should have their attention drawn to considering the question of insurance; see note to *Ord.* 35, *r.* 9, in the *County Court Practice*.

The *County Court Practice* should be referred to.

ADOPTION OF CHILDREN

Applications for adoption are made under the Adoption Act, 1958. The Adoption (County Court) Rules, 1959, apply.

An application for an order authorising the applicant to adopt an infant may be made by a person *domiciled* in England or Scotland (s. 1 (1) of the 1958 Act). An application for a *provisional* adoption order may be made by a person not domiciled in England or Scotland if the applicant intends to adopt the infant under the law of the country where he is domiciled (s. 53).

A person not domiciled in England, Wales or Scotland may apply to the High Court for an adoption order under the Adoption Act, 1968, which brings the United Kingdom into line with the Hague Convention on Adoption of the 15th November, 1965. See *Supreme Court Practice*. Vol. 2.

England in the Adoption Act includes Wales (s. 57 (1)). An infant is a person who has not attained the age of eighteen.

An adoption order may not be made in England unless the applicant and infant *reside* in England (s. 1 (5)), except that s. 12 allows an application to be made by a person who is not ordinarily *resident* in *Great Britain*, in which case the application must be made in the High Court or a county court; the applicant, however, must be domiciled in England or Scotland

An application for an adoption order may be made in the High Court; or, to a county court or a magistrates' court within the jurisdiction of which the applicant or infant resides at the date of the application (s. 9 (1) of the 1958 Act). An

K

application for a *provisional* adoption order may not be made in a magistrates' court (s. 53 (2)).

The infant must have been continuously with the applicants for three months after the age of six weeks before the date of the order (s. 3(1)).

At least three months before the anticipated date of the adoption order (or six months in the case of a provisional adoption order), the applicants must notify the local authority (usually, the Director of Social Services) of their intention to apply unless one of the applicants is a parent of the infant or the infant is above compulsory school age (ss. 3 (2) and 53 (5)).

Requirements:

(a) Originating application in *Form* ACA 1 and copy;

(b) Medical reports of the applicants, except where one of the applicants is a parent of the infant, or the infant has reached the upper limit of compulsory school age (*Form* ACA 3 may be used);

(c) Medical report of infant, except where one of the applicants is a parent or relative of the infant, or the infant has reached the upper limit of compulsory school age (*Form* ACA 4 may be used);

(d) Consent, if any (*Form* ACA 5);

(e) Marriage certificate of applicants;

(f) Birth (or adoption) certificate of infant;

(g) Death certificate of any deceased parent of the infant;

(h) If a request is made to dispense with consent of parent, statement of facts to be annexed to the application;

(i) *Fee:* £1 (No. 2 (i) (b)).

Consent is required of a parent of the infant (not the father of an illegitimate child), of a guardian of the infant, and, on the application of one of two spouses, the consent of the other spouse (s. 4).

The court may dispense with the consent of a parent or guardian, who has abandoned, neglected or persistently ill-treated the infant, or cannot be found or is incapable of giving his consent or is withholding his consent unreasonably (s. 5). There are many decisions on dispensing with consent, which are referred to in the *County Court Practice*. An application to dispense with a consent may be made at the hearing or on an application made before the hearing, according to circumstances.

Where the applicant intends to request the court to dispense with a consent, the request must, unless otherwise directed, be made in the originating application, or if made subsequently, by notice to the registrar. A statement of the facts on which the applicant intends to rely must be attached to the application or notice (*Adoption (C.C.) Rules*, 1959, *r.* 5 (3)).

As to attendance of mother who refuses to give consent, note *Re M. (an infant)* [1972] 3 All E.R. 321.

If an applicant desires that his identity be kept confidential, he may apply to the court office for a serial number before filing the application.

The registrar, of his own motion, appoints a guardian *ad litem*, usually the Director of Social Services, who makes a report, which is confidential, and which is not usually shown to the applicant/s. The application is heard by the judge in chambers.

As to position of putative fathers and adoption by stepparents, note article "Adoption by Stepparents", 117 Sol. J. 606.

An adoption order is drawn up in *Form* ACA 9. If an adoption order is made by a county court in Wales or Monmouthshire in respect of an infant born there and if the adopter so requests, the Schedule to the order is drawn up in bilingual language in *Form* ACA 9W. A copy of the order is sent to the Registrar General for an entry to be made in the Adopted Children Register and an abridged copy of the order in *Form* ACA 10 is sent to the applicant (*Adoption (C.C.) Rules*, 1959, *r.* 20). A copy of an adoption order may not be supplied except:

(*a*) in accordance with the above *r.* 20;

(*b*) at the request of the Registrar General or the applicant or one of the applicants;

(*c*) on the application of any other person under an order of the judge, or

(*d*) in certain circumstances, at the request of another

county court, a juvenile court or the High Court (*ibid, r.* 22).

If an infant, when he has become an adult, wishes to obtain a copy of an adoption order affecting himself, he must obtain an order of the judge. Enquiries have to be made at the county court which made the order as to what procedure should be followed.

BANKRUPTCY

The courts having jurisdiction in bankruptcy are the High Court and certain county courts (Bankruptcy Act, 1914, s. 96).

A list at the end of the *County Court Practice* shows which courts exercise bankruptcy jurisdiction and their districts·

A bankruptcy petition may be presented to the county court for the district in which the debtor has resided or carried on business for the longest period during the six months immediately preceding its presentation (Bankruptcy Act, 1914, s. 98).

The Bankruptcy Rules, 1952, apply.

COMPANIES ACT, 1948

Those county courts which have jurisdiction in bankruptcy also have jurisdiction in companies matters. These courts are shown in a list at the end of the *County Court Practice.*

Where the amount of the share capital of a company paid up or credited as paid up does not exceed £10,000, the county court having companies jurisdiction for the district in which the registered office of the company is situate has concurrent jurisdiction with the High Court to wind up the company (Companies Act, 1948, s. 218).

Winding up

The circumstances in which a company may be wound up by the court are contained in the Companies Act, 1948, s. 222.

A company may be wound up by the court, *inter alia*, if it is unable to pay its debts (s. 222 (*e*)). The definition of inability to pay debts is contained in s. 223.

The Companies (Winding-up) Rules, 1949, apply.

Requirements on presentation of petition for winding up:

(a) Petition in *Form* 4, 5 or 5A of *Companies Winding-up Rules* and three copies, and an additional copy if the company is in voluntary liquidation;

(b) *Fee:* £3 (No. 24 (i)).

Notice of the time and place of hearing are written on the petition and sealed copies (*Rules* 26 and 27).

Affidavit (*Form* 9 or 10) verifying the petition must be sworn after and filed within four days of the presentation of the petition (*Rule* 30).

Other matters

Those county courts which have jurisdiction in winding up also have jurisdiction in other matters under the Companies Act, 1948. Those proceedings, which are required by the High Court rules to be commenced by petition, must be commenced by petition in the county court (C.C.R., *Ord.* 46, *r.* 16). Other proceedings would be commenced by originating application. As to which types of proceeding is appropriate, reference should be made to R.S.C., *Ord.* 102, *rr.* 2 to 5, and notes thereto in the *Supreme Court Practice.* C.C.R., *Ord.* 6, *rr.* 4 and 5, apply to the county court proceedings (applying *Ord.* 48, *r.* 2). For precedents, see Palmer's *Company Precedents.*

Two examples of requirements follow—

Application to extend the time for registration of a charge under s. 101

Requirements:

(a) Originating application (*Form* 23) and copy;

(b) *Fee:* £2 (No. 24 (ii)).

Evidence may be by affidavit containing the information set out in the *Supreme Court Practice,* 1973, at para. 102/2/17. A copy of the affidavit must be served on any opposing party (*Ord.* 20, *r.* 5 (1)). Applications are commonly *ex parte.*

If the application is not made by the company, service must be effected on the company.

Petition to restore a company's name to the register under s. 353 (6)

Requirements:

(a) Petition (*Form* 24) and copy;

(b) *Fee:* £3 (No. 24 (i)).

The Registrar of Companies must be made respondent and served. Where there are assets, notice of the application should be given to the Treasury Solicitor. Service would be by post in any case on filing certificate in *Form* 6.

Evidence in support of or in opposition to a petition may be by affidavit unless the judge otherwise directs (*Ord.* 20, *r.* 3). A copy of any affidavit must be served on the opposite party (*Ord.* 20, *r.* 5 (1)).

See generally, *Supreme Court Practice*, 1973, para. 102/5/36.

BILLS OF SALE

The Bills of Sale Act (1878) Amendment Act, 1882, and the Act of 1878, and the Bills of Sale (Local Registration) Rules, 1960, apply.

A register of bills of sale is kept in a county court of those bills of sale made, that is, granted, by persons residing in its district where the address is outside the London Bankruptcy District, or if the goods are situated within its district. Copies of the bills of sale may be inspected by the public.

Fees: on searching the index, 5p; on inspecting a bill of sale or notice of satisfaction, 5p (No. 23).

DEEDS OF ARRANGEMENT

The Deeds of Arrangement Act, 1914, and Deeds of Arrangement Rules, 1925, apply.

Where the place of business or residence of the debtor who is one of the parties of a deed of arrangement, or who is referred to therein, is situate in some place outside the London Bankruptcy District, the registrar in London of such deeds must within three clear days after registration transmit a copy of the deed to the registrar of the county court in the district of which such place of business or residence is situate (Deeds of Arrangement Act, 1914, s. 10).

The county court keeps a register of the copy deeds sent to it, and the register may be inspected by the public. *Fee:*

on searching the register and on inspecting the filed copy, 15p for each deed (No. 26 (iii)).

Payment into court by trustee of a deed of arrangement.—At any time after the expiration of two years from the date of the registration of a deed of arrangement, the court having jurisdiction in bankruptcy in the district in which the debtor resided or carried on business at the date of the execution of the deed may, on the application of the trustee or a creditor or on the application of the debtor, order that all moneys representing unclaimed dividends and undistributed funds then in the hands of the trustee or under his control be paid into court (Deed of Arrangement Act, 1914, s. 16).

The application may be made in C.C.R. *Form* 23.

The heading of the application would be:

In the   County Court.

No. of Matter

IN THE MATTER OF the Deeds of Arrangement Act, 1914, And in the matter of a Deed of Arrangement between *A. B.* of   and his creditors dated the   day of   19   and registered under the Act on the   day of   19 .

Ex parte *C. D.* Trustee.

Application under s. 7 of the Deeds of Arrangement Act, 1914, *to extend time to register a deed of arrangement.*—R.S.C., Ord. 94, *r.* 4, applies. Application is made by affidavit *ex parte* to a Master in the Q.B.D.

Other applications.—Other than applications under s. 7 of the 1914 Act, applications, which are to be made to the High Court or the county court having jurisdiction in bankruptcy in the district in which the debtor resided or carried on business at the date of the execution of the deed, are deemed to be proceedings in bankruptcy and must be supported by affidavit, except that applications for extension of time for procuring the assent of creditors to a deed under s. 3(1) or for filing the statutory declaration required by s. 3(4) may be made *ex parte* and without affidavit unless the court otherwise orders (*Deeds of Arrangement Rules, r.* 17).

The Deeds of Arrangement Rules, 1925, are set out in Williams on Bankruptcy.

Fees: on an application under the Rules, 25p (No. 26 (ii)); on setting down a motion for hearing before the judge, £1 (No. 26 (iv)).

Form of application under s. 3 to extend time for procuring assent of creditors to a deed

In the   County Court

No. of Matter

IN THE MATTER OF a Deed of Arrangement between *A. B.* of   (*add description*)   and his creditors, dated the   day of   19   , and registered under the Deeds of Arrangement Act, 1914, on the day of   19   .

Ex parte Trustee *C. D.* of

I, the Trustee under the above-mentioned Deed of Arrangement, apply to the Court for an order to extend the time for procuring the assent of creditors to the deed under section 3 (1) of the Deeds of Arrangement Act, 1914 and to extend the time for filing the statutory declaration required by section 3 (4) of the said Act on the following ground:—

Dated this   day of   19

(signed)

[of

Solicitor for] the Trustee.

CERTIFIED BAILIFFS

The Law of Distress Amendment Acts of 1888 and 1895, and Distress for Rent Rules, 1953, as amended, particularly by S.I. 1971 No. 1333 regarding fees and charges, apply.

No person may act as a bailiff to levy any distress for rent unless he is authorised to act as a bailiff by a certificate in writing under the hand of a county court judge (or, subject to rules made under the Act, a registrar) (Act of 1888, s. 7).

Certificates may be general or special. A special certificate

is granted for a particular distress or distresses. A special
certificate may be granted by a judge or registrar, but a
general certificate may be granted only by a judge. A
certificate may not be granted to an officer of a county court,
but any practising solicitor is entitled to one on the payment
of the prescribed fee (Distress for Rent Rules, 1953, *rr.* 2
to 6).

A certificate, otherwise, may be granted to any applicant,
who satisfies the court that he is a fit and proper person to
hold it and gives an undertaking that he will not levy distress
at any premises in respect of which he is regularly employed
in person to collect a weekly rent. An applicant for a general
certificate must satisfy the judge that he is resident or has
his principal place of business in the district of the court,
although, once granted a certificate, he may levy a
distress anywhere in England and Wales. If he is not a
ratepayer rated on a rateable value of not less than £25
per annum, he may be required to give security (*ibid.*,
rr. 7 to 10).

A general certificate remains in effect until the following
1st February and may be renewed for a successive period of
twelve months.

Fees: on application for general certificate, 50p, for a
special certificate, 25p; for renewal, 25p. There are also fees
for approving security (No. 31).

A list of certified bailiffs is exhibited in the court office.

The practice for making applications varies. A suggested
form of application is:—

In the   County Court.

IN THE MATTER OF the Law of Distress Amendment
Acts, 1888 and 1895.

I,   of [*state address and
occupation*] apply to the judge for a general certificate
pursuant to the Law of Distress Amendment Act, 1888,
section 7, and the Law of Distress Amendment Act,
1895, section 3, to act as a bailiff to levy distresses in
England and Wales.

I undertake not to levy distress at any premises in

respect of which I am regularly employed in person to collect a weekly rent.

I do not carry on the business of buying debts.

I am resident [or/and I have my principal place of business] at   in the district of this court.

I have never been refused a certificate or had a former certificate cancelled or declared void [or as the case may be].

I am a ratepayer rated on a rateable value of £
[or as the case may be].

Dated this   day of   19   .

(signed) Applicant

FAMILY PROVISION

The Family Provision Act, 1966, s. 7, gives jurisdiction to county courts to make orders under s. 1 of the Inheritance (Family Provision) Act, 1938, or s. 26 of the Matrimonial Causes Act, 1965, or s. 36 of the Matrimonial Causes Act, 1973, (formerly s. 15 of the Matrimonial Proceedings and Property Act, 1970 where the value of the deceased's net estate does not exceed £5,000.

The 1938 Act enables a dependant of the deceased to apply to the court for reasonable provision to be made out of the deceased's net estate for the maintenance of that dependant. Section 26 of the 1965 Act enables a former spouse of the deceased who has not remarried to make similar application for reasonable provision for the former spouse's maintenance out of the net estate of the deceased. Section 36 of the Matrimonial Causes Act, 1973, enables a party to a maintenance agreement to apply for an alteration of a continuing agreement after the death of the other party. In all cases application must be made within six months from the first grant of representation unless the court permits a later application.

Where proceedings under either Act are commenced in the High Court and it appears to the court that a county court would have jurisdiction, the High Court may order the proceedings to be transferred to the most convenient county court (1966 Act, s. 7 (3)).

Procedure in the county court is regulated by *Ord.* 45A. Application is made in the court for the district in which the deceased resided at his death, or if he was not then resident within England or Wales, in the court for the district in which the respondent or one of the respondents resides or carries on business or the estate is situated, or in any other case in the court for the district in which the applicant resides or carries on business. Application is in *Form* 370 or 370A (not supplied by the court).

Requirements:—

(*a*) Originating application in *Form* 370 or 370A and a copy for each respondent;

(*b*) Official copy of grant of representation and of every testamentary document admitted to proof;

(*c*) In cases under s. 26 of the 1965 Act, sealed copy of decree dissolving or annulling applicant's marriage to the deceased;

(*d*) In cases under s. 36 of the 1973 Act, a copy of the agreement to which the application relates;

(*e*) *Fee* £3 (No. 2 (iv)); where service by bailiff, 50p for every respondent to be served;

(*f*) Legal aid certificate, if any, and notice of certificate for service on respondent (*Ord.* 45A, *r.* 2).

Notice in *Form* 26 with a copy of the application annexed is served. Every respondent must file an answer within twenty-one days after service, with copies thereof to be sent by the court to every other party (*Ord.* 45A, *r.* 4).

The hearing may, if the judge thinks fit, be in chambers (*Ord.* 45A, *r.* 7).

Application for an interim order may be made on notice under *Ord.* 13, *r.* 1 (*Ord.* 45A, *r.* 5).

The personal representatives must produce at the hearing of an application under the Act of 1938 or s. 26 or 27 of the Act of 1965 the probate or letters of administration. If the judge makes an order or an interim order or an order dismissing the application, a sealed copy of the order is sent to the

Principal Registry of the Family Division at Somerset House, Strand, London WC2R 1LP. With the order, the probate or letters of administration are sent so that a memorandum of the order may be indorsed thereon or permanently annexed thereto. A fee of £1 (No. 7 of the Supreme Court (Non-Contentious Probate) Fees Order, 1970) is remitted by cheque payable to the Paymaster-General at the same time. The probate or letters of administration are returned after the memorandum has been made (*Ord.* 45A, *r.* 8).

GUARDIANSHIP OF MINORS

Guardianship of Minors Act, 1971

Ord. 46, *r.* 1, applies.

An application may be made to the county court for the district in which the respondent (or any of the respondents) or the applicant or the minor to whom the application relates resides (s. 15 (1) (*b*)). A county court does not have jurisdiction where any respondent resides in Scotland or Northern Ireland unless the originating process can be served on the respondent in England or Wales (s. 15(3)).

Requirements:

    (*a*) Originating application in *Form* 23 and copy for service;

    (*b*) *Fee*: £1 (No. 2 (1) (*a*)); and for service by bailiff, 50p.

Services must be effected not less than twenty-one clear days before the return day.

Where the application is made under s. 5 of the 1971 Act and the minor has been received into the care of a local authority, service must be effected "not less than fourteen days before the day fixed for the hearing" on the local authority (*Ord.* 46. *r.* 1 (2)).

Rules as to originating applications apply.

The proceedings are heard in chambers unless the court otherwise directs (*Ord.* 46, *r.* 1 (1)).

Marriage Act, 1949

Order 46, *r.* 9, applies to an application under s. 3 of this Act for the consent of the court to the marriage of a minor.

An application may be made to the county court of the district in which any applicant or respondent resides (s. 3(5)).

Requirements:

(*a*) Originating application in *Form* 23 and copies for service;

(*b*) *Fee:* £1 (No. 2 (1) (*a*)); and for service by bailiff, 50p.

Service must be effected not less than seven clear days before the day fixed for hearing on every person whose consent is required and who has refused his or her consent. The application must be heard in chambers unless the court otherwise directs. It may be heard by the registrar. It is not necessary for the applicant to have a next friend (*Ord.* 46, *r.* 9).

HIRE-PURCHASE ACT, 1965

The Hire-Purchase Act, 1965, applies to hire-purchase and conditional sale agreements, and also credit sale agreements, where the total price does not exceed £2,000, but not to those agreements where the hirer or buyer is a corporate body (ss. 2 and 4).

If, in an action to enforce a right to recover possession of goods under s. 35 or before one-third of the price has been paid, the owner or seller claims any sum due under the agreement or contract of guarantee, a county court has jurisdiction to hear and determine it if apart from the section the county court would not have jurisdiction to do so (s. 49).

Order 46, *r.* 10, applies to actions for delivery of goods.

Goods are "protected goods" where:—

(*a*) the goods have been let under a hire-purchase agreement, or agreed to be sold under a conditional sale agreement;

(*b*) one-third of the price has been paid or tendered; and

(*c*) the hirer or buyer has not terminated the bailment (s. 33).

The owner (hire-purchase agreement) or seller (conditional sales agreement) may not enforce any right to recover possession of protected goods from the hirer or buyer otherwise than by action (s. 34).

Subject to certain exceptions all parties to the agreement and any guarantor must be made parties to the action (s. 35 (2)). Where the hirer or a guarantor has not been served, the court may on the *ex parte* application of the plaintiff made at or before the hearing, dispense with the requirement that he be made a party to the action (*Ord.* 46, *r.* 10(1)). An assignor of the plaintiff does not have to be made a party (*Ord.* 46, *r.* 1A).

The court may make an interlocutory order to protect the goods (s. 35(3)). An application for such an order may be heard by the registrar (*Ord.* 46, *r.* 10(2)).

Section 35 (4) provides that the court may make:—

(*a*) an order for the specific delivery of all the goods (judgment in *Form* 139(2)); or

(*b*) an order for the specific delivery of all goods and may postpone the operation of the order on payment of the unpaid balance of the hire-purchase price by instalments (judgment in *Form* 139(3)); or

(*c*) an order for the specific delivery of a part of the goods and for the transfer to the hirer of the remainder (judgment in *Form* 139(4)).

This applies with appropriate modifications to conditional sale agreements (s. 45).

If the offer in an admission by the hirer is accepted, and a guarantor is a party to the action, judgment may not be entered before the return day (*Ord.* 46, *r.* 10(3)).

Where the goods have *not* been returned to the owner during the operation of a *postponed order*, the court may vary the postponement and conditions or revoke the previous order (s. 39). Form of order, *Form* 139 (5).

Where all the goods have *not* been recovered under any order made under s. 35 (4) or s. 39 (1) (*c*), and the order has not been complied with or the hirer or guarantor has wrongfully disposed of the goods, the court may revoke the order and make an order for payment of the *unpaid hire-purchase price* (s. 42). Form or order, *Form* 139 (6).

Where an order has been made under s. 35 (4) (*a*) or (*b*), if all the goods have been recovered, *or* if the court has revoked a postponed order, an application may be made for the payment of a money claim (s. 44). The plaintiff applies under *Ord*. 46, *r*. 10 (6). He applies on notice (*Form* Ex. 23) to the defendant, and, if the claim has not already been made in the action, particulars of the claim must be given in or annexed to the notice. Any additional plaint fee must be paid (*Fee*, No. 27).

Where the owner has begun an action to recover "protected goods" under s. 35, he may not take any step to enforce any payment under the agreement except in that action (s. 41).

After the death of the hirer or buyer, s. 46 and Sched. 3 to the 1965 Act apply. Where a postponed order has been made against a deceased hirer or buyer, notice of an application to issue a warrant of delivery must be served personally on the person in possession of the goods (*Ord*. 46, *r*. 10 (5)).

HOUSING ACTS, 1957 to 1969

In the many proceedings under the Housing Acts, reference must be made to the particular section to determine the type of proceeding to be taken, the period within which proceedings must be taken and the venue. In some instances, the section provides for the appropriate court, and then it is usually the court for the district in which the premises are situated. Otherwise, the venue is determined by *Ord*. 2, *rr*. 13 or 15.

For applications and appeals under Part III of the 1969 Act, see under "Rent Acts", *infra*.

Requirements on an appeal:

(*a*) Request in *Form* 25 for the entry of the appeal and copy for service;

(*b*) Copy of the order, decision or award appealed against;

(*c*) *Fee:* £1.50 (No. 3); and for service by bailiff, 50p.

The title of the matter must include the name of the Act

and should also include the section of the Act under which the proceedings are taken.

Order 6, *r.* 6, applies.

Requirements for an orginating application:

   (*a*) Originating application in *Form* 23 and copy for service;

   (*b*) *Fee:* £3 (No. 2(iv)); and for service by bailiff, 50p.

Order 6, *r.* 4 applies.

For precedents, see McCleary's County Court Precedents.

LANDLORD AND TENANT ACTS, 1927 and 1954

The *Landlord and Tenant Act,* 1927, *Part* I, relates to compensation for improvements of business premises. *Part* II includes s. 19, which contains provisions relating to covenants not to assign or make improvements etc., without consent.

The *Landlord and Tenant Act,* 1954, *Part* I, relates to security of tenure for residential tenants under long leases to enable them in certain circumstances to obtain statutory tenancies after their leases have expired.

The *Landlord and Tenant Act,* 1954, *Part* II, relates to security of tenure for business tenants and enables them in certain circumstances to obtain a new lease after their leases have expired.

Order 40 applies to proceeding under these Acts. Forms of originating application are not supplied by the court. The form of answer (*Form* 336) to an originating application for a new tenancy under the Act of 1954 is supplied by the court.

Jurisdiction.—Under **Part I of the Act of 1954,** jurisdiction conferred on the court is exercised by the county court (s. 63(1)). Part I applies to houses within the same rateable values as the Rent Act, 1968, s. 1.

Under **Part II of the Act of 1954 and Part I of the Act of 1927,** jurisdiction conferred on the court is exercised:

   (*a*) by the county court where the rateable value does not exceed £5,000;

   (*b*) by the High Court, where it exceeds £5,000 (s. 63(2) of the Act of 1954).

Such jurisdiction may by agreement in writing between the parties be transferred from the county court to the High Court or from the High Court to a county court specified in the agreement (s. 63(3)). Such an order for transfer may be made on the application of a person interested (s. 63(4)).

As regards an application for a declaration that consent to assign, etc., was unreasonably withheld, the county court has the same jurisdiction as the High Court (s. 53).

Venue.—An originating application may be commenced in the court for the district in which the respondent, or one of the respondents, resides or carries on business, or in which the subject matter of the application is situated (*Ord. 2, r. 13*).

Normally, the proceedings would be commenced where the property is situated as in the case of proceedings for the recovery of land under *Ord. 2, r. 2*.

Applications.—An application for possession of land under s. 13 of the Act of 1954 is made by ordinary summons and the particulars of claim must contain additional matters set out in *Ord. 40. r. 5*. This section is in **Part 1** of the Act and the jurisdiction of the county court is *not* governed by the rateable value of £5,000.

Otherwise, originating proceedings are usually by originating application. Some forms of originating application are referred to in *Ord. 40*.

Fees: on any originating application under the Act of 1927; or under the Act of 1954, £3 (No. 30); if service by bailiff, 50p for each address (No. 4) unless service is to be effected by post.

In all originating applications under *Ord. 40*, the respondent must file, within fourteen days of service (inclusive of the day of service), an answer with copy or copies for the applicant.

The most common originating application, is that **for a new tenancy under the Act of 1954, s. 24.** The application must be made (that is, filed and proceedings commenced) not less than two nor more than four months after the giving of the landlord's notice under s. 25 or, as the case may be, after the making of the tenant's request for a new tenancy (s. 29 (3)).

L

Requirements:

(a) Originating application in *Form* 335 and copy for each respondent;

(b) *Fee:* £3 (No. 30); and fee for service by bailiff, 50p.

Form 335 is not supplied by the court.

The court draws notice in *Form* 26 to respondent of day of hearing and annexes it to the copy of the originating application for service.

When proceedings were commenced late because the court office was closed, and they were entered by post, see *Hodgson* v. *Armstrong* [1967] 1 All E.R. 307.

The time within which service must be effected is one month unless extended; where reasonable efforts have been made to serve the application and service has not been effected, the registrar may order that the time be extended for a further period not exceeding one month or for successive periods, but the time may not be extended unless application is made within the currency of the preceding period (*Ord.* 40, *r.* 8 (1A)).

The respondent must, within fourteen days of service (inclusive of the day of service), file an answer in *Form* 336 (supplied by the court) with a copy for each of the other parties. The copies are sent by the court to the other parties.

If the respondent landlord is himself a tenant under a lease having less than fourteen years unexpired at the date of the termination of the current tenancy, he must forthwith after service of the application serve a notice in *Form* 341 (supplied by the court) on his landlord, and on any other person having an interest in the property, other than a freehold interest or tenancy, who to his knowledge is likely to be affected by the grant of a new tenancy (*Ord.* 40, *r.* 15 (2) and (6)).

If the applicant is not the immediate tenant of the respondent, he must forthwith after filing the application, serve a notice in *Form* 341 on his landlord (*Ord.* 40, *r.* 14 (2)).

The order is in *Form* 337 and a copy is served on every party. Where the court is precluded from making an order for the grant of a new tenancy on any grounds specified in s. 30 of the Act of 1954, a note is entered in the books of the court stating all the grounds on which the court is precluded

(*Ord*. 40, *r*. 8 (4) and (5)). An application for a certificate under s. 37 (4) is made *ex parte* in *Form* 339, and the certificate is in *Form* 340 (no fee).

The registrar has power to make orders by consent (see *Ord*. 40, *r*. 19).

A joint application under s. 38(4) of the Act of 1954 to the court to authorise an agreement excluding the provisions of ss. 24 to 28 or for the surrender of a tenancy before its natural expiration is made by originating application under *Ord*. 6, *r*. 4, in *Form* 23. *Fee*: £3 (No. 30). An affidavit in support is suitable. Since the order is by consent, the registrar may make the order (*Ord*. 23, *r*. 1). No party has to be served. For precedents, see McCleary's County Court Precedents.

LEASEHOLD PROPERTY (REPAIRS) ACT, 1938

This Act restricts the enforcement of repairing covenants in leases for a term of seven years or more of which three years or more remain unexpired. The Law of Property Act, 1925, s. 146, requires a lessor to serve notice containing certain particulars prescribed by the section before commencing proceedings to exercise a right of re-entry for breach of a covenant to repair. This section does not require any notice when the claim is for damages, but such a notice is made necessary by s. 1(2) of the Act of 1938. Where a counter-notice is served by a lessee on the lessor under s. 1 of the 1938 Act, following the service of such a notice the lessor may commence proceedings to enforce any right of re-entry or forfeiture or for damages without leave of the court.

The court having jurisdiction is the court in which the action for enforcement is to be commenced (County Courts Act, 1959, Sched. I).

Requirements:

Application for leave under s. 1:

(*a*) Originating application in *Form* 23 and copy for service;

(*b*) *Fee*: £3 (No. 2); and for service by bailiff, 50p.

LEASEHOLD REFORM ACT, 1967

This Act enables the tenant of a leasehold house to acquire the freehold or an extended lease of fifty years, in certain circumstances, where the lease is one granted for a term exceeding twenty-one years at a low rent, that is, not exceeding two-thirds of the rateable value. The tenant must have occupied the house as his residence for the last five years or for periods amounting to five years in the last ten years. The rateable value of the house and premises on the appropriate date must not be more than £400 in the Greater London area and £200 elsewhere (s. 1 of the 1967 Act).

Order 46, *r.* 20, applies to proceedings under this Act. No forms of originating application are supplied by the Court. For precedents, see McCleary's County Court Precedents.

The county court has jurisdiction to determine the principal issues under the Act (s. 20), except those relating to management schemes (s. 19). Assessment of the price of the freehold, the rent payable under an extended lease and the amount of compensation, in default of agreement, must be determined by the Lands Tribunal (s. 21).

Venue.—If the proceedings are for the possession of a house, they should be commenced in the county court for the district in which the house is situated (*Ord.* 2, *r.* 2). Otherwise, except for payment into court, the proceedings, it seems, might be commenced in the court for the district in which the respondent, or one of the respondents, resides or carries on business, or where the subject matter is situated (*Ord.* 2, *r.* 13).

Application for possession under s. 17 *or s.* 18 *for possession*
Requirements:

    (*a*) Originating application in *Form* 23 and copy for service;

    (*b*) *Fee:* £3 (No. 2); and for service by bailiff, 50p.

The notice in *Form* 26, which is served on the respondent with the copy originating application, must contain a notice in *Form* 397. The respondent must, forthwith after being served, serve a notice of the proceedings in *Form* 396 on every person in occupation of the property or part of it under an immediate or derivative sub-tenancy (*Ord.* 46, *r.* 20 (4) (*a*)). Forms are not supplied by the court.

The respondent must within fourteen days after being served file an answer stating the grounds, if any, on which he intends to oppose the application and giving particulars of every sub-tenancy, together with a copy for every other party to the proceedings.

The persons on whom *Form* 396 is served may, with leave of the court, appear and be heard in the proceedings. Application could be made under *Ord.* 15, *r.* 10, although this rule applies to actions.

Other originating applications

Requirements:

As for (*a*) and (*b*) above without *Forms* 396 and 397. One of the many applications which may be made under the Act is an application by the landlord under Sched. 3, para 4 (1) for leave to bring proceedings to enforce a right of re-entry or forfeiture where the tenant has made claim to acquire the freehold or an extended lease.

Payment into court under s. 11(4) *or s.* 13(1) *or* (3)

Order 46, *r.* 20(2), applies.

The appropriate court for payment in is the court for the district in which the property is situated, or, if the payment is made by reason of a notice under s. 13(3), the county court named in the notice.

Requirements:

(*a*) Affidavit containing information required by *Ord.* 46, *r.* 20(2) (*a*);

(*b*) Money to be paid into court.

No fee seems to have been prescribed.

The court sends notice of payment to the landlord and to every person named in the affidavit.

On a subsequent payment into court by the landlord under s. 11(4), he files an affidavit and notice is sent to the tenant and persons named in the affidavit.

Any application to deal with money would attract a fee of 50p (No. 8).

RENT ACTS

Rent Act, 1965

The main provisions of the Rent Act, 1965, have been repealed, except Part III. Part III deals with protection against harassment. It also prohibits eviction without a court order of a person who occupies a dwelling, subject to a tenancy or employment occupancy which is not statutorily protected.

Rent Act, 1968

This Act consolidates the previous Rent Acts (except Part III of the 1965 Act). Section 1 defines a protected tenancy. Section 7 defines a regulated tenancy and sets out what is a controlled tenancy.

Section 1, as amended by the Counter-Inflation Act, 1973, s. 14, provides that a tenancy under which a dwelling-house is let as a separate dwelling is a protected tenancy:—

    (a) unless its rateable value on the 1st April 1973 exceeded, in Greater London, £1,500, or, elsewhere, £750 (besides exceeding certain lesser values before that day); or

    (b) unless s. 2 applies to the tenancy; or

    (c) unless under ss. 4 or 5 the tenancy is precluded from being a protected tenancy by reason of the body in whom the landlord's interest is vested (i.e. the Crown or a local authority, etc.).

The jurisdiction of the county court is contained in s. 105 of the Act. The powers conferred under this section include the making of orders for possession where the Act applies. The section also permits a county court to deal with claims arising out of the Act notwithstanding that the amount of the claim would otherwise be outside its jurisdiction. Section 105(4) provides that, if a person takes proceedings in the High Court which he could have taken in a county court, he will not be entitled to costs. Section 11 deals with the suspension of orders for possession.

The most common procedure under the Rent Act is an action for possession, to which the normal county court procedure applies.

Rent (County Court Proceedings) Rules, 1970

These rules apply to certain applications under the Rent Act, 1968, and to appeals and applications under Part III of the Housing Act, 1969. These applications and appeals must be commenced by originating application in the court for the district in which the premises are situated, except that, if the question to be decided arises in county court proceedings, it may be determined in those proceedings (*Rule* 3(1)).

Costs are taxed on Scale 1 of Appendix B of the County Court Rules, unless the court otherwise directs. The costs may be fixed (*Rule* 3(8)).

Application for leave to distrain

Requirements:

(*a*) Originating application (*Form* 6 (Rent Act)) and copy (form supplied by the court);

(*b*) *Fee:* 5p for every £1 or part thereof of the amount to be distrained, maximum 50p (No. 32) (no fee for service).

Notice of hearing in C.C.R. *Form* 26, prepared by the court, with copy of the originating application annexed, is served on the respondent not less than four clear days before the hearing (*Rule* 3 (3)). Service may be by post and also by the rent collector (*Rule* 3(4)).

The application is heard by the registrar, normally in chambers. The order is in *Form* 7 (Rent Act).

Other applications

Rule 3 of the Rent Rules applies.

Requirements:

(*a*) Originating application and copy for service;

(*b*) *Fee:* 50p (No. 32) (no fee for service).

The appropriate form of originating application is provided for in the Appendix to the Rent Rules. Notice of hearing is in C.C.R. *Form* 26, prepared by the court. Notice of hearing with a copy of the originating application annexed is served on the respondent not less than ten clear days before the hearing. Service may be by post. Any answer, with a copy for the applicant, should be delivered to the court office within eight days of service. The application may be heard by the registrar, except that an application under paras. 3 or 7 of Sched. 1 of the Rent Act, 1968, must in the first place be heard by the judge. The hearing may take place in court or in chambers.

The Appendix to the Rent Rules contain the forms of order which must be served on all parties.

Three examples of applications follow.

Application by landlord for cancellation of a certificate of disrepair

Section 52(3) and Sched. 9, paras. 4(6) and (7) and 6(3) of the Rent Act, 1968, apply. The procedure is as above.

Form of application is *Form* 18 (Rent Act), supplied by the court. The local authority is not made a respondent under para. 4(6) and (7) unless the court otherwise directs (*Rule* 3(9)). A copy of the order in *Form* 19 (Rent Act) is served on both parties and on the local authority.

Application to determine a question relating to a tenancy, such as whether a tenancy is a protected tenancy

Section 105 of the Rent Act, 1968, applies. Form of application is *Form* 24 (Rent Act) and form of order is *Form* 25 (Rent Act). The procedure is as above.

Application for order to local authority to issue qualification certificate or for cancellation

Section 49 of the Housing Act, 1969, applies. The procedure is as above.

Form of application is *Form* 26 (Rent Act). The local authority must be made a respondent unless the court otherwise directs. Form of order is *Form* 27 (Rent Act). The order is served on all parties.

Proceedings for compensation under s. 19 of the Rent Act, 1968

Proceedings are commenced by plaint and, if the judgment complained of was obtained in a county court, the action must be brought in that court (*Rule* 4).

LEGITIMATION

The Legitimacy Act, 1926, and the Matrimonial Causes Act, 1973, s. 45, formerly the Matrimonial Causes Act, 1965, s. 39, apply. *Order* 39 applies.

It should not be overlooked that a copy of the originating application for a declaration of legitimation and a copy of the affidavit in support must be sent by registered post (or delivered) to the Attorney-General not less than one month before the application is filed (*Ord.* 39, *r.* 7). It should be addressed to him at the office of the Treasury Solicitor, 3 Central Buildings, Matthew Parker Street, London, SW1H 9JS.

Venue.—Proceedings may be commenced in the court for the district:—

(a) in which the applicant resides; or
(b) in which the marriage leading to the legitimation occurred; or
(c) in Westminster County Court, if neither the residence of the applicant nor the place of marriage is situated in England or Wales (*Ord.* 39, *r.* 1(2)).

Requirements:

(a) Originating application in *Form* 323 and copies for service;
(b) Affidavit in *Form* 325 and copies for service;
(c) Every birth, death or marriage certificate intended to be relied on at the hearing;
(d) Any legal aid certificate and notices of certificate for service;
(e) *Fee:* £3 (No. 2); and for service by bailiff, for each respondent to be served, 50p.

If the applicant does not reside in England or Wales, the application must show an address for service in England or Wales (*Ord.* 39, *r.* 3).

If the applicant is an infant, the affidavit in support is made by his next friend (*Ord.* 39, *r.* 5).

Notice of hearing is drawn by the court and is in *Form* 324.

A sealed copy of the application and affidavit and notice of hearing must, unless the court otherwise directs, be served by bailiff not less than twenty-eight clear days before the hearing on every respondent (except the Attorney-General) personally. The judge may dispense with service on any respondent if the judge is satisfied that he cannot be found.

Notice of hearing in *Form* 326 is sent to the Attorney-General to give him not less than twenty-eight clear days' notice of the day fixed for hearing (*Ord.* 39, *r.* 8).

A respondent may file an answer within fourteen days of the service. Every answer, which contains matter other than a simple denial of the facts, must be accompanied by an affidavit made by the respondent verifying such other matter. There must be filed with the answer and affidavit copies of them for all other parties (*Ord.* 39, *r.* 9).

The order is in *Form* 328. An order transferring an application to the High Court is in *Form* 329.

LIMITATION ACT, 1963

Order 46, *r.* 8, applies. Requirements before commencement of action:

(a) Originating application in *Form* 23;
(b) Affidavit exhibiting copy of proposed particulars of claim;
(c) Fee: £3 (No. 2(iv)).

The hearing is before a judge in chambers. There is no respondent.

Requirements after commencement of action:

(a) Notice of application in *Form* Ex. 23 and copy;
(b) Affidavit and copy for service;
(c) *Fee:* 50p. (No 8).

The hearing is before a registrar. *Order* 13, *r.* 1, applies.

MAINTENANCE ORDERS

The Maintenance Orders Act, 1950, provides for the registration of a maintenance order made by a county court under the Guardianship of Minors Act, 1971, (as well as in matrimonial proceedings) in a court of summary jurisdiction in Northern Ireland or the sheriff court in Scotland. *Order* 46, *r.* 14, applies. *Fee:* 25p (No. 29(i)).

The Maintenance Orders Act, 1958, enables an order for maintenance made in a county court under the Guardianship of Minors Act, 1971 (as well as in matrimonial proceedings), to be registered in a magistrates' court for enforcement. *Order* 46, *r.* 17, applies. *Fee:* 25p (No. 29(i)).

MARRIED WOMEN

Law Reform (Husband and Wife) Act, 1962

In an action in *tort* brought by one party to a marriage against the other during the subsistence of the marriage, the jurisdiction of the court under s. 1(2) of this Act of 1962 may be exercised by the registrar (*a*) if the action is to be heard by the judge, at any time before the hearing, or (*b*) if the action is to be heard by the registrar, at any stage of the proceedings. The registrar must, after the time for filing a defence has expired, consider whether the power to stay the action should be exercised and must fix a day for preliminary consideration under *Ord.* 21 (*Ord.* 46, *r.* 7).

Married Women's Property Act, 1882, s. 17

Order 46, *r.* 11, applies to proceedings under the Married Women's Property Act, 1882. Proceedings under s. 17 may be commenced in the county court in the district of which either party resides. A county court has jurisdiction irrespective of the value of the property.

Requirements:

(*a*) Originating application in *Form* 23 and copy for service;

(*b*) *Fee:* £3 (No. 2); and if service by bailiff, 50p;

(*c*) Legal aid certificate, if any, and notice of certificate for service.

The notice in *Form* 26 to the respondent of the hearing contains a notice in *Form* 395 requiring the respondent to file an answer and a copy for each other party within fourteen days of service (inclusive of the day of service). The notice is referred to by the court as *Form* 26 (MWPA). The registrar sends the copy answers to the other parties.

The judge may refer the application to the registrar who then has power to hear and determine it. The first hearing may be for giving directions. For form of order for selling a house, see *Re Draper's Conveyance* [1967] 3 All E.R. 853.

Matrimonial Homes Act, 1967, s. 1

A county court has jurisdiction irrespective of the rateable value (*ibid.* s. 1 (6)).

Order 46, *r.* 19, applies.

Requirements:

    (*a*) Originating application in *Form* 23 and copy for
       service;

    (*b*) *Fee:* £3 (No. 2); and if for service by bailiff, 50p;

    (*c*) Legal aid certificate, if any, and notice of certificate
       for service.

Where the application is for an order terminating the
respondent's rights of occupation and it appears that the
respondent is not in occupation of the dwelling-house and his
whereabouts cannot be ascertained, the registrar may dispense
with service on him on an *ex parte* application by the applicant
(*fee*, 50p) (*Ord.* 46, *r.* 19(3)).

The proceedings must be heard and determined in chambers
unless the court otherwise directs and may be heard by the
registrar (*Ord.* 46, *r.* 19(1) and (2)).

The same procedure applies to an application for an order
vacating the registration of a land charge of Class F (*Ord.* 46
r. 19 (4)).

RACE RELATIONS ACT, 1968

Where the Race Relations Board is unable to secure a
settlement of any differences or a satisfactory assurance against
the repetition of an allegedly unlawful act, they may bring an
action for an injunction, damages or a declaration, and for a
revision of a contract which contravenes the Race Relations Act.

The county courts having jurisdiction under the Act are
appointed under the County Courts (Race Relations
Jurisdiction) Order, 1968, which sets out the enlarged districts
for the purpose of the Act.

The proceedings are commenced by ordinary summons. They
may be commenced in the court for the district, as defined in
the above Order of 1968, in which:—

    (*a*) the defendant resides or carries on business; or

    (*b*) the act or any of the acts in respect of which the
       proceedings are brought took place (*Ord.* 2, *r.* 11).

The judge must be assisted by two assessors appointed from
a list prepared by the Lord Chancellor (*s.* 19(7) of the Act).

The County Court Practice should be referred to, which also lists the county courts which have jurisdiction under the Act.

FUNDS

The County Court Funds Rules, 1965, apply.

Invested Funds

The following are the most usual funds subject to investment by the court:

Infants' settlements (s. 174 of the Act) and *Ord*. 16, *r*. 13 (order made in the High Court) and *Ord*. 5, *r*. 19 (order made in a county court);

Trustee Act, 1925, s. 63.

The money is placed on deposit account and attracts 4% interest (*Funds Rules* 16 and 23). The registrar may transfer money on deposit to a short-term investment account which attracts interest at the rate of 8%, or to a long term investment account under the Common Investment Funds Scheme, 1965.

There are three common funds under the Scheme:

(1) The Capital Fund designed to increase capital value as opposed to securing a high annual return. Dividends are paid on the 15th November and 15th May after deduction of income tax.

(2) The High Yield Fund for beneficiaries to whom income is more important than capital appreciation. Dividends are paid on the 1st October and 1st April after deduction of income tax.

(3) The Gross Income Fund for beneficiaries to whom income is more important and who have little or no liability for income tax. Dividends are paid on the 1st February and 1st August in full without deduction of income tax. Not more than £5,000 should be invested in this fund for any one beneficiary, whose income should not exceed £400 per annum, in view of the fact that tax is not deducted.

The prices of units in these funds are quoted in *The Times* under "Funds in Court" in the column of "Unit trust prices".

In the case of "infants' settlements", notice of payment into court is sent to the person interested in *Form* Ex. 82, to which is attached a notice explaining the scheme of investment. This form is sent also in the case of funds paid in under s. 174, instead of the prescribed form, *Form* 97.

Applications for dealing with the fund and for payment out are usually made by a party in person or his parent. Applications are made without fee by letter or on a form supplied by the court, *Form* Ex. 33. An appointment is given for attendance before the registrar. In the case of the Trustee Act, 1925, s. 63, *Ord*. 38, *r*. 2, applies (see, *supra*).

Fee (other than under *Ord*. 38 (Trustee Act)): £1 for every £100 or part thereof, maximum £10 (No. 61). This fee is deducted from the money paid into court.

ADMINISTRATION ORDERS

Where the whole debts of a judgment debtor do not exceed £1,000, the court may make an administration order in respect of them. The order provides for the debtor to pay his debts in full or to such extent as under the circumstances appears to the court to be practicable. The debtor pays instalments into court.

Sections 148 to 156 of the Act and the Administration Order Rules, 1971 apply.

The debtor applies on *Form* AO 1, which is supplied by the court. This form lists the debtor's creditors and the amount of each debt and sets out his means.

An administration order may be made under the Attachment of Earnings Act, 1971, s. 4, on an application for an attachment of earnings order. In this case, the debtor completes *Form* AO 2.

Notice of hearing is sent to the creditors. The application may be heard by the registrar. There must be at least one judgment debt.

When sufficient money has been paid into court, a dividend is declared and the creditors notified (Administration Order Rules, 1971, r. 24).

An attachment of earnings order may be made to enforce the order.

The administration may be revoked on the grounds set out in AO *Rule* 18, for example, where two or more instalments are in arrear.

The order is administered and enforced by an official of the court.

COSTS (*Ord.* 47)

General

Costs are usually in the discretion of the court (*Ord.* 47, *r.* 1). Scales of costs are set out in Appendix B to the Rules. The registrar is the taxing officer (*Ord.* 47, *r.* 3). Costs must be taxed except (*a*) when allowed in Appendix D (*fixed* costs of summons, judgment, etc.), or (*b*) when allowed on the Lower Scale, or (*c*) when a solicitor for the party, in whose favour costs are given, wishes them to be *assessed* (Appendix E then applies), or (*d*) when awarded in respect of an application and not included in the general costs of the action, or (*e*) when agreed in lieu of taxation (*Ord.* 47, *rr.* 35 to 37). When Appendix D applies, only the costs therein are allowed, unless the judge or registrar otherwise orders (*Ord.* 47, *r.* 36 (1)).

In proceedings brought on behalf of a person under disability, the costs must be taxed (*Ord.* 5, *r.* 19 (4)).

As to costs recoverable by a layman acting in person, note *Malloch v. Aberdeen Corporation* [1973] 1 All E.R. 304.

For scales of *fixed* and *assessed* costs, see Appendix I to this book.

Scales of costs (Ord. 47 r. 5)

No solicitors' costs are allowed as between party and party when the sum of money does not exceed £75, unless a certificate is granted under *Ord.* 47, *r.* 13 (see below), or unless the sum exceeds £5, in which case there may be allowed the costs stated on the summons, and the costs of enforcing any judgment or order and, also, such costs as in the opinion of the court have been incurred through the unreasonable conduct of the opposite party in relation to the proceedings or the claim made therein.

There are one Lower Scale and four Higher Scales:

Exceeding	£5 and up to £20	..	Lower Scale
,,	£20 ,, ,, ,, £50	..	Scale 1
,,	£50 ,, ,, ,, £200	..	,, 2
,,	£200 ,, ,, ,, £500	..	,, 3
,,	£500	.. .. ..	,, 4

Money claims (Ord. 47, r. 6)

The scale of costs in an action for *money only* is determined:

(a) costs of the plaintiff, by the amount recovered;
(b) costs of the defendant, by the amount claimed;
(c) costs of a third party, by the amount claimed against him;
(d) costs payable by a third party, by the amount recovered against him.

These do not apply in equity proceedings, Admiralty actions or actions in which the title to hereditaments comes into question.

Counterclaims (Ord. 47, r. 7)

The above applies to counterclaims subject to the following:—

Where in one action a claim for money only and a counterclaim for money only are tried—

(a) if the plaintiff is awarded costs on both claim and counterclaim, the costs are on the scale applicable to what he recovers on the claim, but if the claim is less than the counterclaim, the costs subsequent to the filing of the counterclaim are on the scale applicable to the counterclaim; and

(b) if the defendant is awarded costs on both claim and counterclaim, the costs are on the scale applicable to the amount he recovers on the counterclaim or the amount of the plaintiff's claim, whichever is the larger, but the costs prior to the filing of the counterclaim are on the scale applicable to the claim;

provided that the costs of work done solely in connection with the claim shall be on the scale applicable to the claim and the costs of work done solely in connection with the counterclaim are on the scale applicable to the counterclaim.

The general principles are laid down in *Medway Oil and Storage Co. v. Continental Contractors* [1929] A.C. 88. See Miscellaneous Notes on costs in the *County Court Practice*. A special order may be necessary to avoid injustice as to the incidence of costs respecting claim and counterclaim.

Money paid into court (Ord. 47, r. 8)

Where money in court is accepted in satisfaction of the cause of action in respect of which it was paid, and another cause remains to be tried, then the costs subsequent to the date of the payment into court are, unless the registrar when taxing or fixing and allowing the costs otherwise directs, determined by the amount recovered or claimed in respect of the cause of action remaining to be tried.

Where money is paid into court and the plaintiff does not accept it in satisfaction of his claim or of the cause of action in respect of which it was paid, the costs incurred after the date of the payment into court are on the scale which would have been applicable if no money has been paid into court, or on such lower scale as the court or the registrar, when taxing or fixing and allowing the costs, may determine having regard to any saving of expense effected by reason of the payment into court. This paragraph applies where money is paid to the plaintiff in satisfaction or an account of the plaintiff's claim as it applies where money is paid into court.

Transfer from High Court (Ord. 47, r. 9)

In proceedings transferred from the High Court, where the amount remaining in dispute at the date the action is set down in the county court is less than the amount originally claimed, the costs incurred after that date are taxed on the scale applicable to the amount remaining in dispute.

Garnishee proceedings (Ord. 47, r. 12)

The scale is determined as follows:

(a) costs of the judgment creditor, by the amount recovered; and

(b) costs of the garnishee, or the judgment debtor, by the amount claimed by the judgment creditor.

M

Companies Act, 1948 (*Ord.* 47, *r.* 14)

Other than winding up proceedings, costs under the Companies Act, 1948, are on the scale of costs applicable to similar proceedings in the High Court.

Other proceedings (*Ord.* 47. *r.* 15)

In other proceedings, such as for recovery of land, and in most originating applications, the judge may award costs on such scale as he thinks fit, provided that, where notice of discontinuance has been given, the registrar has power on taxation to determine the scale. This power may be exercised by the registrar in cases heard or tried by him (*Ord.* 48, *r.* 5 (1)).

Most county courts have a practice of allowing costs in "possession cases" on one specified scale, unless there is reason for awarding it on some other scale.

Difficult questions of law or fact (*Ord.* 47, *r.* 13)

In any proceedings in which the judge certifies that a difficult question of law or a question of fact of exceptional complexity is involved, he may award costs on such scale as he thinks fit.

This power may be exercised by the registrar in cases heard or tried by him (*Ord.* 48, *r.* 5 (1)).

Certificate for increased charges (*Ord.* 47, *r.* 21 (2) to (5))

Where the costs of any proceedings are on one of the Higher Scales and the judge is satisfied from the nature of the case or the conduct of the proceedings that the costs which may be allowed may be inadequate in the circumstances, he may direct that the registrar on taxation shall not be bound by the amounts appearing in the scale in respect of the following items: 1, 2, 5, 6, 7, 8, 18, 26, 29 and 30.

When such a direction has been given, the registrar may, if he thinks fit, allow on taxation such larger sums as he thinks reasonable.

Where the costs are on Scale 3 or 4, the registrar, if no contrary direction has been given by the judge, may on taxation increase these items on being satisfied as to the same matters.

If a certificate is not given at the hearing, an application may be made afterwards on notice. The notice must be served on the other party within fourteen days of the making of the order awarding costs or within fourteen days of the receipt of notice of payment into court or of notice of discontinuance. Where an application which could have been made at the hearing is made subsequently, the judge may refuse the application on the ground that it ought to have been made at the hearing.

Counsel

There is no provision in the Lower Scale for a fee for counsel.

No fee for counsel is allowed on taxation in respect of an interlocutory application, unless the judge or registrar certifies that the application is fit for counsel (*Ord*. 47, *r*. 19).

Unless the judge otherwise orders, no fee for counsel with brief shall be allowed in an action for recovery of money only:—

(a) where the defendant has admitted the whole or part of the claim within fourteen days (inclusive of the day of service) and the plaintiff recovers judgment for no more than the amount admitted; or

(b) where no defence has been delivered and the defendant does not appear at the hearing to resist the claim (*Ord*. 47, *r*. 20).

Where the costs are on Scale 2, 3 or 4, the judge may certify that the proceedings are fit for the employment of more counsel than one (*Ord*. 47, *r*. 21 (1)).

Where a party appearing by counsel is awarded costs, but not costs for counsel, he may be allowed the costs for appearing by solicitor (*Ord*. 47, *r*. 27).

Witnesses (*Ord*. 47, *rr*. 29 to 34A)

The allowance for a witness is such sum as the judge or registrar thinks reasonable, not exceeding that in Column 2 of Appendix C to the Rules (see Appendix II to this book), but that sum, unless the court otherwise orders, may not exceed Column 1 of Appendix C where a witness has lost no earnings, or the period during which the witness has been away does not exceed four hours. The registrar may allow larger sums on taxation where costs are on Scale 3 or 4 (*Ord.* 47, *r.* 29). In addition, a witness may be allowed travelling and hotel expenses (*Ord.* 47, *r.* 31).

As to expert witness, *Ord.* 47, *r.* 30, applies.

Taxation (*Ord.* 47, *rr.* 38 to 41)

A party may ask for his costs to be assessed (*Ord.* 47, *r.* 37 (2) and (3)). If the costs are not assessed at the hearing, they may be applied for by letter, setting out the costs required—court fees, witnesses, costs for service by solicitor, for certificate for postal service or substituted service, and the suggested allowance under Appendix E. A form (*Form* (N)) for this purpose is set out in the *County Court Practice*, 1973, p. 861.

If costs are agreed, and a party wishes to make them part of the record, a direction to that effect can be made at the hearing. If not made at the hearing, the registrar should be informed by letter, and then a *fee* (No. 19 (ii)), 25p, is payable in lieu of a fee for taxation.

A bill of costs for taxation should be lodged within fourteen days of the order for costs, with all necessary vouchers and papers, if required. A copy of the bill with notice of appointment must be served on the other party one clear day before the appointment. *Order* 47, *r.* 38 (4), provides for when the bill is not lodged within the proper time. The provisions are not always enforced. Fee on taxation, see Appendix III to this book.

After taxation, the court sends to the party who is ordered to pay the costs notification in *Form* Ex. 74 (not prescribed) if he did not attend or was unrepresented.

Where costs are taxed in accordance with the provisions of Sched. 3 to the Legal Aid and Advice Act, 1949, an allocatur in *Form* Ex. 80 (not prescribed) is issued by the court.

Taxation of costs awarded by tribunal

An application for the taxation of any costs, fees or expenses

which, pursuant to any Act or statutory instrument other than
the County Court Rules, fall to be taxed by a county court is
made by originating application (*Ord.* 47, *r.* 41). It would be
issued in the court for the district in which the respondent
resided or carried on business (*Ord.* 2, *r.* 13). *Order* 6, *r.* 4, also
applies.

Requirements:
- (*a*) Originating application in *Form* 23 and copy for
service;
- (*b*) Bill of costs and copy for service to be annexed to
originating application;
- (*c*) *Fee:* see Appendix III to this book; it is fee No. 2(iii)
calculated on the amount allowed and is exactly the
same as the fee (No. 19(i)) paid on a normal taxation.
A note to the fee states that a deposit for the full fee
should be made at the time of entering the application.
No fee for service if served by post.

For precedents of originating application, see McCleary's
County Court Precedents.

The application is made to the registrar and the taxation
becomes the hearing. The court sends a certificate of the result
of the taxation to every party.

Notes to *Ord.* 47, *r.* 41, in the *County Court Practice* list some
of the proceedings to which the rule applies.

Costs ordered to be paid by an Industrial Tribunal may be
taxed in a county court and the order must give directions as to
the scale (*Industrial Tribunals (Industrial Relations, etc.)
Regulations*, 1972, S.I. 1972 No. 38, *r.* 13(4)).

Costs of proceedings in the National Industrial Relations
Court are taxed in the High Court.

Value added tax

Where litigation is in the course of a plaintiff's business
and he is able to deduct the V.A.T. paid on solicitors' services,
or where litigation is conducted by a plaintiff's salaried solicitor,
an allowance for V.A.T. does not arise.

The relevant rules are *Ord.* 47, *rr.* 18 and 37(6). *Order* 47,
r. 18, provides that on taxation there may be allowed as a

disbursement a sum equivalent to value added tax in so far as the tax is not deductible as input tax by that party. *Order* 47, *r.* 37(6), provides that where costs are assessed or fixed and allowed without taxation under para. (1), (2) or (4) of *Ord.* 47, *r.* 37, the above *Ord.* 47, *r.* 18, will apply.

These paragraphs do not apply to the fixed costs in Appendix D to the C.C.R., that is, costs on summons, on entering judgment by default, etc. However, *Ord.* 47, *r.* 36(1), provides that Appendix D applies "unless the judge or registrar otherwise orders". Therefore, if V.A.T. is required to be added to fixed costs an order of the registrar or court is required.

It is suggested that courts may make an order if a certificate, similar to that used in the High Court in V.A.T. cases, is filed.

The certificate might be in the following form:

(*Heading*)

With reference to the costs in this action, I [we] certify that the Plaintiff would not be entitled to recover value added tax on such costs as input tax pursuant to s. 3 of the Finance Act, 1972.

Dated

(*signed*) Solicitor for Plaintiff.

Objections and review

The procedure is set out in *Ord.* 47, *r.* 42.

Any party dissatisfied with the taxation of any costs by the registrar may apply to him to reconsider the taxation.

The application may be made on the day of taxation; if it is not made then, it must be made on notice. *Order* 13, *r.* 1, applies. Notice of application can be in *Form* Ex. 23. No fee. The notice must be filed within two days of the taxation and operates as a stay of execution of the costs. The notice must specify the items in respect of which the application is made and the grounds and reasons for the objections.

On the hearing the registrar must, if requested by either party, state in writing the reasons for his decision.

Any party who is dissatisfied with the registrar's decision on his reconsideration may apply to the judge for a review. The application for review may be made on the same day. If it is not made then, it must be made on notice. *Order* **13**, *r.* **1**, applies. Notice of application can be in *Form* **Ex. 23**. *Fee:* 50p (No. 20). The notice must be filed within two days of the reconsideration and operates as a stay of execution of the costs. The notice must specify the items in respect of which the application is made and the grounds and reasons for the review. The judge may, without any application of any party, appoint two assessors, one of whom must be a registrar (see *Ord.* **47**, *r.* 42 (6)).

Where a party has legal aid, an application for objections and review requires the authority of the appropriate area committee of The Law Society (see *Legal Aid (General) Regulations*, 1971, *reg.* 23 (6) to (11)).

DUPLICATE PLAINT NOTE

An application for a duplicate plaint note is made by affidavit in *Form* 378 (supplied by the court) (*Ord.* 48, *r.* 19 (2)). *Fee:* 15p (No. 68).

TIME

When a period of three days is prescribed, no Sunday or day on which the court office is closed is included (*Ord.* 48, *r.* 10).

Subject to the provision of the rules, any time fixed by the County Court Rules may be enlarged or abridged by consent or by the court on application (*Ord.* 13, *r.* 5).

CHANGE OF SOLICITOR

Order 48, *r.* 11, applies.

When a party desires to change his solicitor, he or the new solicitor must give not less than forty-eight hours' notice to the registrar and to every other party (*Ord.* 48, *r.* 11 (3)).

Where a party, for whom a solicitor has acted, desires to act in person, he must give notice to the registrar and to every other party. Where notice is not given, the solicitor who has ceased to act must apply on notice for an order declaring that he has ceased to act (*Ord.* 48, *r.* 11 (5)). *Order* 13, *r.* 1, applies to the application. Form of application may be in *Form Ex. 23.* If the application is made before the hearing, the fee is 50p.

Notice of change is in *Form 371* as follows:

(Heading)

TAKE NOTICE that I,

who have hitherto employed   of

as my solicitor in

the above-mentioned action or matter have ceased to employ him and that my present solicitor is

of

whose address for service is

or

TAKE NOTICE that I, the undersigned   [*name and address of new solicitor*]   have been appointed to act as solicitor for the above-named plaintiff   [*or* defendant] in the place of   [*original solicitor*]   and that my address for service is:—

JURIES

County Courts Act, 1959, ss. 94 and 96, Courts Act, 1971 ss. 31 to 40, and *Ord.* 13, *r.* 14, apply.

A trial is without jury in the following cases:

(*a*) Admiralty proceedings;

(*b*) Rent Act proceedings;

(*c*) Appeals under the Housing Act, 1957.

In other proceedings, a trial is without a jury unless the court otherwise orders. If there is a charge of fraud against the party applying or a claim for libel, slander, malicious prosecution, false imprisonment or seduction is in issue, and an application is made for such, an order for trial by jury must be made unless the court is of opinion that the trial requires any prolonged examination of documents or accounts or any scientific or local investigation which cannot conveniently be made with a jury (s. 94).

An application for an order for trial with a jury is made on notice stating the grounds of the application and given not less than ten clear days before the return day, if time allows; but see *Ord.* 13, *r.* 14.

Trial with a jury in county courts is rare.

APPENDIX I

ABBREVIATED TABLE OF SOLICITORS' COSTS

In claims for money only, where the sum of money does not exceed £75, no solicitors' charges may be allowed unless—

   (*a*) a certificate is granted under *Ord.* 47, *r.* 13;

   (*b*) the sum exceeds £5, in which case there may be allowed—

      (i) the costs stated on the summons;

      (ii) the cost of enforcing any judgment or order;

      (iii) such costs as in the opinion of the court have been incurred through the unreasonable conduct of the opposite party in relation to the proceedings or the claim made therein (*Ord.* 47, *r.* 5(4)).

Item	Over £5 to £20	Over £20 to £100	Over £100 and for possession of land
	£	£	£
Issue of summons	1·50	3·00	6·00
Postal service, *add:*	0·25	0·25	0·25
Issue of summons, solicitor's service	2·00	4·00	7·00
Judgment: In default (default summons)	0·50	1·00	1·50
Offer accepted			
Hearing—admission filed			
Hearing—ordinary summons, no defence or admission filed; liquidated demand, delivery of goods, suspended possession orders	1·00	2·00	4·00

	LOWER SCALE Over £5 to £20	SCALE 1 Over £20 to £50	SCALE 2 Over £50 to £200	SCALE 3 Over £200 to £500	SCALE 4 Over £500
	£	£	£	£	£
Trial—assessed costs (Appendix E) ..	3–8	5–10	10–15	15–25	15–40
Attachment of earnings order, or judgment summons for each hearing	1·00	2·00	2·00	2·00	3·00
Execution— issue ..	nil	0·50	0·50	0·50	0·75

APPENDIX II

WITNESS ALLOWANCES
(Appendix C to the Rules)

Class of Person	COLUMN 1 Sum to be paid or tendered at time of service of witness summons	COLUMN 2 Maximum sum per day allowable on taxation
	£	£
Professional persons, and owners, directors or managers of businesses	4·00	10·00
Police officers	3·00	3·00
Clerks, artisans, labourers, and all other persons	1·50	4·00

APPENDIX III
ABBREVIATED TABLE OF FEES

Plaint Fee (No. 1)

For money:

		£
Not exceeding £3		0·75
Over £3 to £6		1·25
,, £6 to £9		1·50
,, £9 to £10		1·75
,, £10 to £11		1·90
,, £11 to £12		2·05
,, £12 to £13		2·20
,, £13 to £14		2·35
,, £14 to £15		2·50
,, £15 to £16		2·65
,, £16 to £17		2·80
,, £17 to £18		2·95
,, £18 to £19		3·10
,, £19 to £20		3·25
,, £20 to £30		3·50
,, £30 to £100		4·00
,, £100 to £200		5·00
,, £200		6·00

Add:

Bailiff's service (No. 4) for each address or for each personal service .. ..   0·50

Limited company is served by post, no fee

Postal service .. ..   Nil

For "infant" settlement .. ..   1·00

For recovery of land only.. ..   4·00

do.   with money claim ..   4·00 plus 10p for every £ or part. Maximum, £5.

For delivery of goods only ..   As for money claim, assessed on value or unpaid H.P. price.

do.   *with* money claim ..   As for money claim, value or unpaid H.P. price and money claim added together.

do.   money claim *in alternative*   As for money, assessed on larger sum.

For any other remedy or relief ..   £5 (except under Rent (County Court Proceedings) Rules).

Note: Where two or more claims are joined, the maximum is £5.
  Add: in all the above, fee for bailiff's service as for money claim.

Originating application or petition (No. 2) includes Married Women's Property Act, 1882, s. 17.   £3.

Exceptions:

(*a*) adoption order, or Guardianship of Minors Act, 1971, or Marriage Act, 1949.   ..   ..   ..   £1.

(*b*) recovery of money awarded by tribunal, *Ord.* 25, *r.* 7A   ..   ..   5p for every £2 or part; minimum 50p, maximum £3.

(*c*) taxation of costs awarded by tribunal, *Ord.* 47, *r.* 41   25p where amount allowed does not exceed £5; where it exceeds £5 but not £100, 5p for every £1 or part thereof; where it exceeds £100, £5 plus 5p for every £2 or part thereof over £100.

(*d*) Landlord and Tenant Acts, 1927 and 1954 (No. 30) ..   £3.

(*e*) Rent Rules (No. 32)—
   (i) for leave to distrain..   5p for every £ or part; maximum, 50p.

   (ii) otherwise   ..   ..   50p.

(*f*) Companies Act, 1948 (No. 24)—
   (i) Petition   ..   ..   £3.
   (ii) Originating application ..   ..   ..   £2.
   (iii) Otherwise   ..   ..   25p.

(*g*) Solicitors Act, 1957, taxation of bill of costs (No. 34)   As exception (*c*) above.

Appeal to a county court (No. 3) (except under Rent (County Court Proceedings) Rules, 1971)   £1·50.

For service by bailiff (No. 4) other than originating application for adoption order or under Rent Rules.   50p. for each person to be served; if personal service not required, then for each address.

Transfer from High Court (No. 17) ..   ..   £2·00.

Amendment
Amended *præcipe* (No. 5) ..   15p.
Service by bailiff (when not by post) (No. 4 (ii))   ..   25p.

Second or subsequent successive summons or matter (No. 6)	50p.
Witness summons (No. 63) ..	10p.
Add: when bailiff's service (No. 4)	50p.
Taxation of costs (No. 19)	
On taxation	25p where amount allowed does not exceed £5; where it exceeds £5 but not £100, 5p for every £1 or part thereof; where it exceeds £100, £5 plus 5p for every £2 or part thereof over £100.
On agreed costs in lieu of taxation	25p.
Application to judge to review	50p.
New order (No. 11)	
Application by plaintiff .. (*Ord.* 24, *r.* 17 or 19)	25p.
Enforcement of judgments	
Warrant of execution (No. 38)	25p for every £2 or part; minimum, 75p maximum, £10.
To re-issue under *Ord.* 25, *r.* 25 (2)	25p.
To re-issue to new address ..	No fee.
Warrant for possession only (No. 47 (i))	£2.
Warrant for possession and money (No. 47 (ii)) ..	£2, plus 20p for every £2, or part; maximum, £5.
Warrant of delivery (No. 48)	25p for every £2 or part of value of goods or balance of H.P. price; maximum £5.
Judgment summons (No. 50)	20p for every £2 or part; maximum £3; plus 50p for every defendant to be served by bailiff.
Second or subsequent successive judgment summons (No. 51)	15p, plus 25p if amended for service by bailiff.
Issue of order of commitment, i.e., the warrant (No. 53)..	5p for every £1 or part; minimum, 50p; maximum £3.
Transfer under *Ord.* 25, *r* 48 (No. 52)	15p.
Garnishee summons (No. 54)	5p for every £1 or part; maximum, £5; plus 50p for every garnishee to be served personally by bailiff.

Application for charging order on land (No. 46)	50p.
Applications for attachment of earnings order (No. 22)—	
(i) to secure maintenance payments	50p.
(ii) to secure judgment debt	
Not exceeding £10 ..	£1.
Over £10 to £20	£2.
„ £20 to £30	£3.
„ £30 to £50	£4.
„ £50 to £100 ..	£5.
„ £100	£6.
(iii) Search in register (No. 22 (iv))	25p.

APPENDIX IV

FORM OF NOTICE OF APPLICATION

(*Form* Ex. 23) (Not prescribed)

In the   County Court

Plaint No.

Between   *Plaintiff*

and   *Defendant*

TAKE NOTICE that I intend to apply to the Judge [or Registrar] of this Court at

on   the   day of   , 19   , at
o'clock for [an order that] [leave to]
[The grounds of this application are] *or*

[An affidavit of   filed this day [a copy of which accompanies this notice] will be read at the hearing in support of this application].

Dated this   day of   , 19

(Signed) [*Plaintiff*] [*Defendant*]

To the Registrar of the Court
and to the [*Defendant*] [*Plaintiff*]

INDEX

N

JUDGMENT—*continued*
 drawing up of, 75
 enforcement of, by charging order, *see* CHARGING ORDER
 in default, 44
 inferior courts, of, extension, 123
 interlocutory, 48
 payment after, 78
 registration of, 77
  cancellation of, 78
 setting aside, 128–130
  absence of defendant, 129
   default action, 129
   failure of postal service, 130
  irregularity, for 130
  new trial, application for, 128–129
       order for, 128, 129
       principles of grant of, 129
 suspension of, 78
 variation of, 78

JUDGMENT CREDITOR—
 application to suspend or vary judgment,79

JUDGMENT DEBT—
 attachment of earnings, *see* ATTACHMENT OF EARNINGS ORDER

JUDGMENT DEBTOR—
 application to suspend or vary judgment, 78
 examination of, 81
  costs, 82
  service, 82

JUDGMENT SUMMONS, 98–103
 costs, 101
 county court jurisdiction in respect of, 99–100
 fees, 101
 hearing of, 101
  non-attendance at, 102
 order of commitment, issue of 102–103
        suspension of, 103
 service, 100
 successive, 101
 transfer of proceedings, 100

JURISDICTION, 2–8
 Admiralty, 4
 ancillary, 6
 consent or agreement as to, by memorandum, 7
 contract, 2
 counterclaims, 6
 equity proceedings, 3–4
 exceeded, 7–8
 land, to recover, 2
 Landlord and Tenant Acts, 150–151
 mortgaged land, possession of, 2
 none, transfer to High Court, 61